FAST FORWARD

HOW HKS SHAPES THE FUTURE OF DESIGN

By William Richards

ORO Editions
Publishers of Architecture, Art, and Design
31 Commercial Blvd, Suite F
Novato, CA 94949

www.oroeditions.com
info@oroeditions.com

Published by ORO Editions

Throughout my career, I have witnessed transformation in the architecture and design industries. I have been fortunate enough to play a small part in that transformation as leader of the American Institute of Architects and the Design Futures Council, and in my role as an educator. As a writer and publisher, I have had the immense privilege of sharing stories about the adaptation and resilience designers demonstrate in our ever-changing world.

For decades, I have seen HKS embrace change. I have seen the firm's designers, thinkers, and innovators face volatility head-on rather than turn their backs on challenges.

This book was conceived as a vehicle for addressing the many rapid evolutions facing us and to showcase how HKS envisions the future, guided by lessons of the past and present. They see the future as brimming with opportunities, and they are taking charge, creating a new and different approach to design driven by research, technology, and creativity. This book is a testament to passion and drive: it showcases the work of a design firm that has a coherent view about the future and what design can do to shape it for the better.

On these pages, we learn from HKS about the positive force that design can be. Their culture of continual improvement, service, and leading by example is evident. I think HKS' vision and mission are akin to a leadership game plan; the firm is comprised of people who understand that to lead is to innovate and vice versa. The pages in this book describe how the firm thinks non-linearly about dilemmas and reinvents process and space, underscoring the value of their ideas. They show us some work that many would consider edgy, not just last year's success formulas.

I had a conversation with a member of HKS' staff recently, a designer who joined the firm not very long ago. When I asked her about the firm's culture, she said, "It's a new reality." I could tell that her experience was different—something completely new—compared to her prior firm.

And that's just it—HKS imagines a new reality. The firm doesn't want to toss aside the successes they and their counterparts in the industry have had, they want to draw upon them and craft designs that lift people up even when economics, materials, and divergent opinions attempt to get in the way. It should be no surprise that sometimes this point of view veers away from conventional wisdom. HKS brings home the point that no firm outperforms their own aspirations. They are one of the most respected design firms in the world, and this book proves that the firm's vision is both expansive and motivating. Indeed, it seems clear that they are poised to take on what is next.

Beyond being a respected design firm, what else is HKS?

First, I'll say that HKS is a truly unique organization. For instance, they understand that in addition to being in the design business, they are a team of communicators and storytellers. They use engaging action vocabulary and design commentary to amplify the *why* behind their solutions and intended outcomes. Scan the headlines in this book and it will become apparent how HKS teams organize design thinking and communication to teach and to lead. They carefully yet precisely use narratives to build bridges using their own brand of unifying business logic. While their work spans the globe, and their projects span many sectors, they are consistently able to clearly illuminate that their work is driven by purpose.

HKS is also an interdisciplinary organization. Design quality is enriched because it is the product of many talented minds working together in concert. HKS projects are executed and completed by integrated professional teams that openly share information and ideas. This approach enables them to increase efficiency and productivity and elevates the notion that diversity of talent leads to better design. The firm frequently embeds research into the design process and measures outcomes to validate and adjust their ideas for future projects. Inquiry is at the heart of their way of operating, and the firm's leaders are developing and using innovative technologies that will enable all disciplines to work with more rigor, simultaneously and interactively. As new technologies industry-wide change design deliverables from lines on paper to integrated databases, the commentary in this book reveals HKS is a firm prepared for strategic use of digital tools including artificial intelligence.

Finally, HKS is a global organization that puts its values front and center. The firm is trusted as a design and real estate service provider working in a 24-7 environment that finds the best people for today's jobs and develops tomorrow's leaders. I know firsthand that HKS places a premium on its talent and the firm's people hold one another accountable for doing what's right. My Georgia Tech Master of Architecture students often seek summer internships at HKS; they describe the firm and its culture as highly functional and exciting—one that is at the champion level of bringing together novel ideas and real-world solutions. Talent practices in some organizations can often be stuck in the last century, where the bottom line and a winner-takes-all mentality drive every decision. HKS unifies talent with the priorities of clients and the people who will use the spaces they design. Simply, HKS realizes the competitive advantage of human capital. It is no secret that firms who put people first are the real winners.

HKS is often held up as a role model in design and real estate circles, wherein I have become friends with the firm's CEO and Chairman, Dan Noble over the years. His vision to carry a firm that began as a small Dallas-based practice by Harwood K. Smith in 1939 forward as a global leader of design excellence is no small feat. He and his predecessors have established HKS as a company with a strong brand that is relevant and prepared for the future. I believe that brand strength is the culmination of promises made—both implicit and explicit—and what the firm stands for. HKS is strong because it stands for collaboration, excellence, and innovation.

Those of us fortunate enough to be a part of the design community know that experience really matters. How will people feel when they walk through a space? How does the context of a building affect how we perceive it, how we live our lives within it? How does design influence our environment and things we see, touch, and engage with? These are questions HKS designers ask themselves with every project they endeavor upon—questions that you'll find answers to within these pages.

In this book, HKS shows us the impact of great design, how it can last for generations, and how the future of design is ours to create together. If HKS is imagining a new reality, it's a reality that I want to live in. If you are looking for your footing in a fast-paced, changing world, this is the book for you.

James P. Cramer, Hon. AIA, Hon. IIDA

Georgia Institute of Technology College of Design, Atlanta, GA
Northern State University Cramer Center for Design and Innovation, Aberdeen, SD

DESIGNING A SINGULAR EXPERIENCE AT EVERY SCALE

Foreword by Dan Noble, CEO and Chairman of HKS

At HKS, we nurture a culture of fearless curiosity. We are creators who relentlessly push the boundaries of what's possible, exploring new ideas, solutions, and advancements without fear of failure. Art, music, stories, inventions, and architecture all possess the power to inspire and affect change—consequential expressions of our best thinking—bridging cultures, languages, and perspectives. They also foster a sense of shared community defined by unity and oneness. Great designers, like the ones I work with, are unafraid to create an architecture of real consequence.

Our view of what a designer can—and should do—has expanded since my first day at HKS four decades ago. Research has become an integral component of how we design, as have all the social sciences. In the end, architecture is not just a functional jigsaw puzzle. It is meant to be awe-inspiring with emotion and experience at its core. That's what makes design such a powerful act. With that power comes the responsibility to think critically, explore deeply, and to leave places better than we found them.

A few years ago, many of the leaders at HKS met to discuss the future of our industry and our role within it. We sought to explore and share the values that truly matter to us, identifying our unique offerings to our clients and the world. We focused our thinking on developing a strategic plan that would act as a catalyst for greater impact and resonance within our global firm. We asked ourselves: What if this were a strategic plan for our lives, not just our business? Would this approach create more meaningful and resonant thinking for our entire firm? Could there be a business case for this line of thinking? We embarked on a journey to let this plan be a vision for our lives, not just our business. This new perspective allowed us to begin discussions on what is truly important to us, both in life and in business.

In exploring our core values, we agreed that relationships form the foundation of who we are. We've been fortunate to work in cities worldwide with clients who have become friends, sharing a common vision that has forged partnerships. Many of these relationships have spanned decades, during which we've found ways to improve people's lives together. Our relationships—with each other, our families, our clients, our partners, and our communities—motivate us to strive higher. Through learning and sharing, we build trust, and in trusted relationships, we are free to innovate and explore new ideas, technologies, materials, and processes that enhance the design, construction, and functionality of our buildings and spaces. We value collaboration and are committed to building a better world together.

As individuals, we hold our personal character in high regard, with authenticity at the core of our values. We expect honesty, humility, and fairness in our interactions, striving to forge meaningful relationships with our clients and partners. While we all have egos, it is collaboration and inventiveness that drive our process. We love what we do and enjoy working with others. Our pride in a job well done is shared with everyone. It's a better way to design and a better way to live.

Our purpose, both individually and collectively, is to deliver beautiful design work that lifts the spirits of all who experience it and addresses complex issues at the heart of the human condition and building performance. Reflecting on why we chose an education in the design field, many of us sought to use our creative intelligence to create positive change in the world. The potential to realize this has never been greater. Our world is rapidly changing and we aim not just to adapt to that change but to help shape it. That's why we've gathered some of the brightest minds from allied industries to research and develop new ideas and methods.

While experimentation is central to our culture, we also focus on studying outcomes to determine what works and where improvements can be made. Outcomes are the currency of credibility. We are committed to creating end products that are both useful and of high value. Beauty without purpose, form without function: these are incomplete design solutions. We aspire to be a design-focused, knowledge-based practice that begins every client interaction with a vision supported by advisory competence, formalizing outcomes upfront in all our work.

Our knowledge is multidisciplinary, blending elements of art, science, technology, and human psychology. We have concentrated on understanding the human condition by developing research in several areas. We study how the brain works and how environments influence health. We are dedicated to resilient and sustainable design that minimizes energy consumption. Understanding the business of our clients in all our practices is essential to our approach. We aspire to make their businesses better.

One major consideration in building a better future is designing for greater equity and inclusion. HKS was among the first architecture firms to join the UN Global Compact, an agreement between the United Nations and global organizations challenging us to look at everything we do—from how we run our company to the places we design—to make the world healthier, more equitable, and sustainable for all. We have a moral imperative to play a substantial role in the health of our planet in its broadest definition. We view this moment as a chance for renewal and reinvention.

Our impact extends beyond the places we design to how we practice design and the teams we collaborate with. We believe inclusion drives creativity and that innovation arises from an engaged, collaborative culture where people draw on their diverse life experiences to generate a variety of rich and differentiated ideas. Through our people-first framework, we commit to building an international design practice that reflects the diversity of the clients, cultures, and communities we serve.

As responsible stewards of our resources, communities, and planet, we are committed to a climate-positive future. Driven by the goal to help limit global temperature rise to below 1.5°C, we, as a firm, achieved carbon neutrality in 2023. Carbon neutrality is a milestone on HKS' journey to net zero. We are building a pathway to eliminate operational carbon from 100 percent of our active design work by 2030 and to reduce the net carbon emissions from our business operations to as close to zero as possible.

The world and our industry face many challenges. Today's risks to architecture involve a complex interplay of environmental, social, economic, and technological factors. From climate change and economic uncertainty to cyber threats and technological obsolescence, to demographic shifts and health and safety concerns, we navigate a complex world amplified by constant change. We believe this complexity requires a responsive and adaptable culture.

Traditionally, the Architecture/Engineering/Construction industry has been slow to innovate, with much written about this sluggish evolution. But we believe we are at a tipping point, on the verge of a quantum leap in the evolution of our industry. Through advanced technology and machine learning, the roles, responsibilities, and tasks of designers will be reinvented, bearing little resemblance to what we know today. Across our industry, what can be commoditized will be commoditized, and what can be automated will be automated. As for us, we'll be part of the discussion on what should be automated, ensuring that human creativity remains at the heart of our process as we forge our path forward.

We are committed to exploring technologies like AI and machine learning to understand how best to leverage them in our work. Venture capital is flowing into our industry, bringing unprecedented potential for innovation, disruption, and competition. Investment in technology will help us work better and smarter, but it cannot replace the ingenuity and spark of genius that reside within the human spirit. That is the foundation of what we do. Our minds and our ability to solve complex problems are our greatest assets.

So where does that leave us?

We believe it sets us on a path to becoming more innovative and stronger partners in developing design solutions and tackling the world's most pressing issues. Creative thinking will help us stay ahead and remain relevant as more of our services become commoditized and automated. We are uniquely equipped to solve the world's most challenging problems that require cross-disciplinary collaborative teams. If we apply this skill set to these problems—whether environmental, societal, behavioral, or spatial, on a macro or micro scale—we will create more fully realized solutions. We will become advisory partners to our clients, opening new avenues for design thinkers to develop a value proposition in great demand.

Good design is good business and can achieve much more than what is immediately apparent. As a firm, we've gone beyond sticks and bricks to drive positive change for the people whose lives unfold in and around those sticks and bricks.

This book represents some of our latest thinking, explorations, and representative work. It delves into how we harness the power of design to enhance the built environment and improve lives, how research and knowledge lay the foundation for great design, and how our work extends beyond the built environment to address some of the most compelling and complex challenges of our day.

ADVANCING DESIGN IMPACT

Good design rises to meet our everyday needs, but great design improves our shared world. Designers strive to create connections that improve our individual experiences, inspiring us and forging the vital links that make our communities thrive. Designing for those experiences is a cornerstone of HKS' practice—what their principals call designing for "beauty and outcomes," one of the firm's three guiding pillars across its twenty-nine global offices.

We all know what beauty is when we see it, but what is its relationship to outcomes? Design that focuses on achieving specific results for the people who will benefit from it—and those who might benefit from it one day—is the basis of outcome-based design, and it means creating spaces that meet basic needs for our well-being. For HKS, that's a beautiful thing, even if we can't always see it.

Positive outcomes have the power to transform communities, and HKS prioritizes human-centered design to create spaces that encourage interaction and engagement. By integrating community needs into their projects, HKS promotes inclusivity and supports well-being, ultimately enriching the fabric of community life.

For the design teams at HKS, improving our shared world means balancing the needs of their clients, the communities these projects serve, and the environment we all must preserve. For them, improving our world is about designing for how people experience the built environment and how it enables them to thrive. Outcomes-based design for people and the planet is a transformational force that, when you see it happen, you can never forget it.

A ROOF THAT PERFORMS: SoFi Stadium's roof shelters upwards of 100,000 visitors and promotes passive cooling with more than 300 panels made of a durable plastic called Ethylene Tetrafluoroethylene (ETFE) that resists corrosion and impacts. The panels outperform glass for insulation and have a fritted pattern that reduces heat so they can help keep fans cool or warm, depending on weather conditions. Several panels are operable and can be adjusted to take advantage of prevailing coastal breezes and pull cooler air into the stadium. The ETFE is also LED-enabled and can display live events happening inside the stadium which can be seen from the air by passengers traveling through LAX.

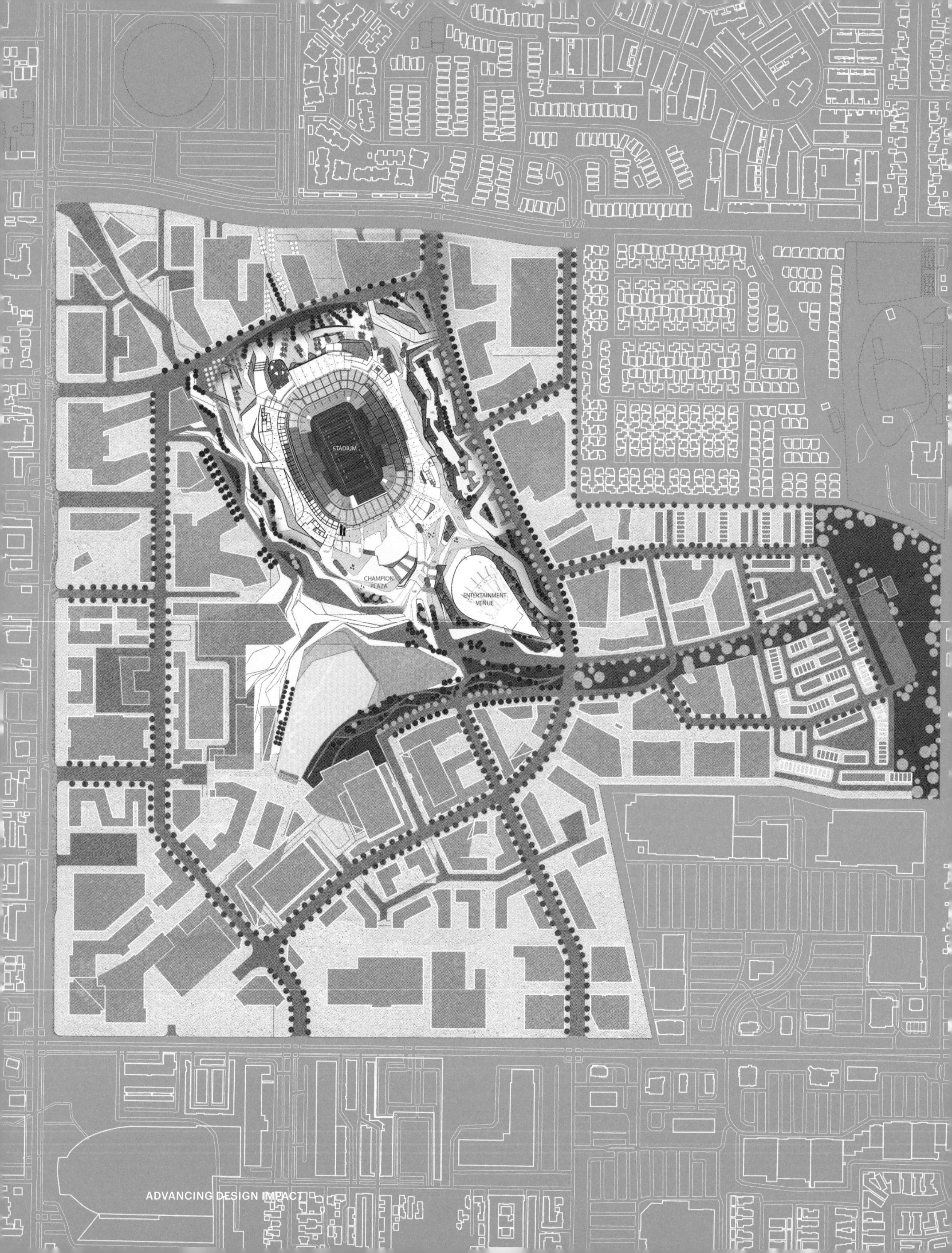
STADIUM
CHAMPION PLAZA
ENTERTAINMENT VENUE

HKS designed SoFi Stadium and Hollywood Park, a marvel sports and entertainment complex in Inglewood, California, featuring three venues under one soaring roof canopy: a stadium, a theater, and a public plaza. SoFi Stadium is the home of the Los Angeles Rams and Los Angeles Chargers, and it's the first football stadium built in the region since the Los Angeles Memorial Coliseum was completed in 1923. But, SoFi Stadium is not just about football. Adjacent to the stadium, the 6,000-seat YouTube Theater is designed for a more intimate entertainment experience with a three-story façade that features a sweeping balcony that overlooks the 2.5-acre American Airlines Plaza, enhancing events at SoFi Stadium.

Offering these types of auxiliary environments alongside the main stadium is central to HKS' commitment to fostering community connections for the 107,000 people who live in Inglewood, alone, nevermind the 9.6 million people in Los Angeles County. By diversifying the kinds of spaces for private or public events such as festivals, concerts, celebrations, or events that have nothing to do with football, the firm ensures the broadest range of uses for this community anchor.

Spanning 3.1 million square feet, the stadium itself seats about 70,000 people, making it the largest in the NFL. In addition to hosting games for the Rams and Chargers, SoFi Stadium hosted Super Bowl LVI in 2022 and the College Football Championship Game in 2023. In 2028, it will host athletic events and ceremonies at the 2028 Olympic and Paralympic Games. Fans who arrived to these and other events have been greeted by a monumental Infinity Screen by Samsung that weighs more than two million pounds—the equivalent of eighty school buses, all gassed up—and spans 120 yards to give everyone in the stadium a front row seat to its 4K LED screen. Beyond the screen, the stadium features several impressive engineering achievements. The field level is dug 100 feet down into the earth—a solution that accommodates the flight path of Los Angeles International Airport (LAX) located three miles away and creates a one-of-a-kind landscape for arriving fans.

Open concourses and landscape canyons offer more than a way for fans to move around. They create opportunities for discovery outside the main event. The billowing roof evokes sails and wings in fitting tribute to its proximity to both nearby marinas and to LAX. SoFi Stadium's expansive landscape also draws in local evergreens like pines and cypresses, hearty olive and fig trees, and scrubby vegetation perfectly suited for the climate and the context.

SoFi Stadium's design team at HKS drew on decades of stadium innovations around the world, but what they created could have only been built in

AN INGLEWOOD DESTINATION: SoFi Stadium and Hollywood Park is a 298-acre sports and entertainment destination in Inglewood, California, just south of Los Angeles. The project includes SoFi Stadium, YouTube Theater, and American Airlines Plaza, as well as twenty-five acres of public space including landscaped parks, trails, and a lake.

tadium

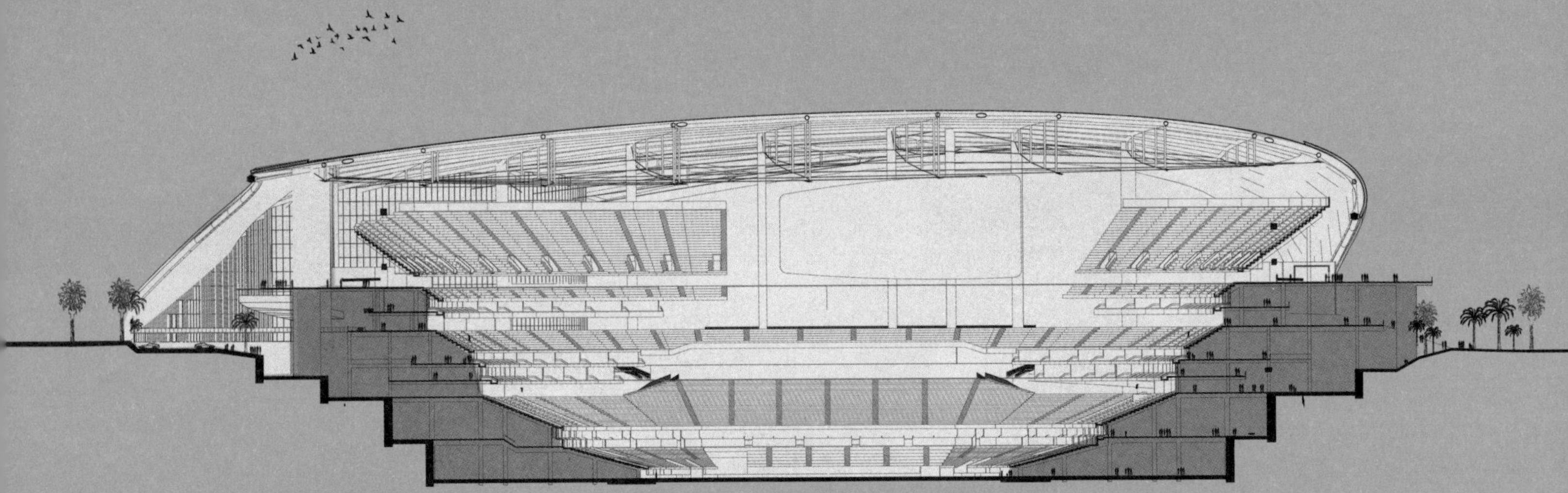

INTEGRATED WITH THE LAND: The stadium is carved into its site so it can meet Federal Aviation Administration height regulations necessitated by its proximity to Los Angeles International Airport (LAX). In collaboration with landscape design firm Studio-MLA, HKS designed a series of canyons with native southern California plants through which fans enter the seating bowl. The heart of the stadium, its playing field, sits 100 feet below grade.

Southern California: something uniquely rooted in this climate, tailored to the needs of this community who can enjoy games and performances in a range of venues including a state-of-the-art theater, event plaza, and, of course, the stadium, itself. In 2024, the American Institute of Architects recognized SoFi Stadium and Hollywood Park with an AIA Architecture Award, an annual prize celebrating the best contemporary design. The jury cited HKS' innovative structural design and ambitious program as key factors, as well as its contribution to a storied landscape.

"I came out to Southern California as a Texan for a specific reason, which is this climate, this environment, and the openness and networks of spaces," says Lance Evans, Venues Design Director and a principal at HKS, "It became about designing a series of design elements that evolved into the park—that was the essence of the project—and we used that as a way to organize the other elements of the site's plan."

Evans explains that the site lies on an active fault line and the nearby air traffic-imposed height limits for the team, two hyper-local conditions that created technical challenges. Yet, the stadium's long-span cable truss roof structure created the kind of stability needed, while also reducing steel tonnage by more than thirty percent compared to a similar building with a different stabilizing solution.

In the end, the greatest challenge was the project's greatest asset: the formidable culture of design and entertainment of L.A. itself.

"We spent a lot of time understanding the fabric of Los Angeles, and from an experiential standpoint, we looked out at best-in-class experiences and we thought about our own great memories of food and wine and culture, too," says Evans. "We also looked at architectural precedents—and our search from the beginning was about creating an invention. Something that could exist nowhere else."

Half a century ago, the historian Reyner Banham wrote about the balance architects have always tried to strike when settling California's coast between a "peculiar pattern of many-centered growth" and a delicate ecology in the foothills west of the El Segundo dunes. From the earliest pueblos and ranchos to the space-age sprawl of Los Angeles International Airport to the new SoFi Stadium, our ambitions for a lush California idyll have always been—and always will be—in a design dialogue with the wild desert communities that sustain us.

RAMS
Pregame Show
RAMS
RAMS

DESIGN AND DELIVERY INNOVATION: SoFi Stadium features 35,000 incredibly thin, anodized aluminum panels, each one uniquely made to promote air flow with more than twenty million small cuts. To ensure the panels and roof structure could be built as designed, architects worked with the California State Architecture Board to develop a custom digital authentication tool and data repository that supported a direct-to-fabrication workflow. Developed in collaboration with Zahner, the panels have a "Frost White" finish that minimizes glare for air traffic from nearby LAX. The panels are also recyclable, so when they reach the end of their sixty-year lifespan, they can contribute to a "cradle-to-cradle" sustainability strategy.

SoFi Stadium

MOODY
OUTPATIENT
CENTER

SUSTAINABLE APPROACHES: By selecting prefabricated panels for the façade of the Moody Outpatient Center at Parkland Hospital, the HKS team was able to reduce the project's carbon footprint as well as its construction timeline and costs. Sustainability and high-performance goals were central to the project, which earned LEED Gold Certification.

Often when we think about communities that sustain us, we think about the importance that healthcare plays in our lives, the doctors and providers we rely upon. The design of our healthcare system is also a dialogue between our needs, however routine or acute they might be, and the herculean logistics required to provide comprehensive care.

Parkland Health has been Dallas County's primary treatment center for more than a century and even if you've never been there, you've probably heard about it as the hospital where President John F. Kennedy's body was taken after his assassination a few days before Thanksgiving in 1963. To say that Parkland is part of the fabric of American life–and certainly Dallas' history–is an understatement. Knowing how high the stakes were, HKS approached the commission for the new Moody Outpatient Center with one objective: create a community anchor for another century.

By consolidating twenty-four clinics across Parkland Health's campus, HKS created an outpatient center that uses state-of-the-art technologies and realizes efficiencies in treatment that help patients heal faster. And the firm did it all in just thirty-four months, which is about half the time of the national average for hospital construction projects–aided by the use of prefabricated panels, which were also cost-effective and reduced the embodied carbon footprint of the building during construction.

The Moody Outpatient Center can welcome up to 800 patients every day across dozens of exam rooms to diagnose and treat severe injuries, as well as therapeutically treat cancer, diabetes, orthopedic ailments, and sexually transmitted infections including HIV. The Parkland Hospital Moody Center for Breast Health, located within the Center, is also crucial for the community, offering accessible care for breast health issues. It provides advanced diagnostic services, early detection screenings, and personalized treatment plans, empowering individuals to manage their health. By emphasizing education and support, the clinic reduces anxiety and stigma, while also promoting community awareness and outreach, ultimately enhancing overall health and well-being.

The Center represents significant community outcomes for Texas by enhancing access to quality healthcare services, fostering early diagnosis and treatment (which improves health outcomes and reduces hospitalizations), and emphasizing preventive care and education. By serving diverse populations and addressing specific community needs, the center strengthens its local and regional healthcare infrastructure, ultimately contributing to the overall well-being and resilience of Texas communities.

The design highlights a story about bolstering the county's safety-net hospital for its most disadvantaged residents, which the HKS and Parkland Health teams did in two key ways. First, by making the outpatient center supremely accessible and easy to use, no matter how patients arrived and no matter what they needed by way of treatment. Second, the HKS design team improved the operations of a hospital center, which was vitally important to retain talented doctors and staff.

"Our focus was on access to care and eliminating barriers," says architect Brian Briscoe, a principal at HKS, who says the team observed the current states of other clinics to identify challenges that could be solved with a new outpatient clinic and developed a clinic "module" approach that helped standardize the operations of two dozen individual clinics. "This was about

DESIGN FOR WELL-BEING: Moody Outpatient Center's design emphasizes individual comfort and well-being in all clinical spaces and public areas. The building incorporates biophilia with organic shapes and textures, a therapy garden and landscaped walking paths. One of many multispecialty clinics within the building, the Moody Center for Breast Health includes open and private waiting areas as well as soothing interior design elements.

1A

MOODY
OUTPATIENT
CENTER

MOODY OUTPATIENT CENTER

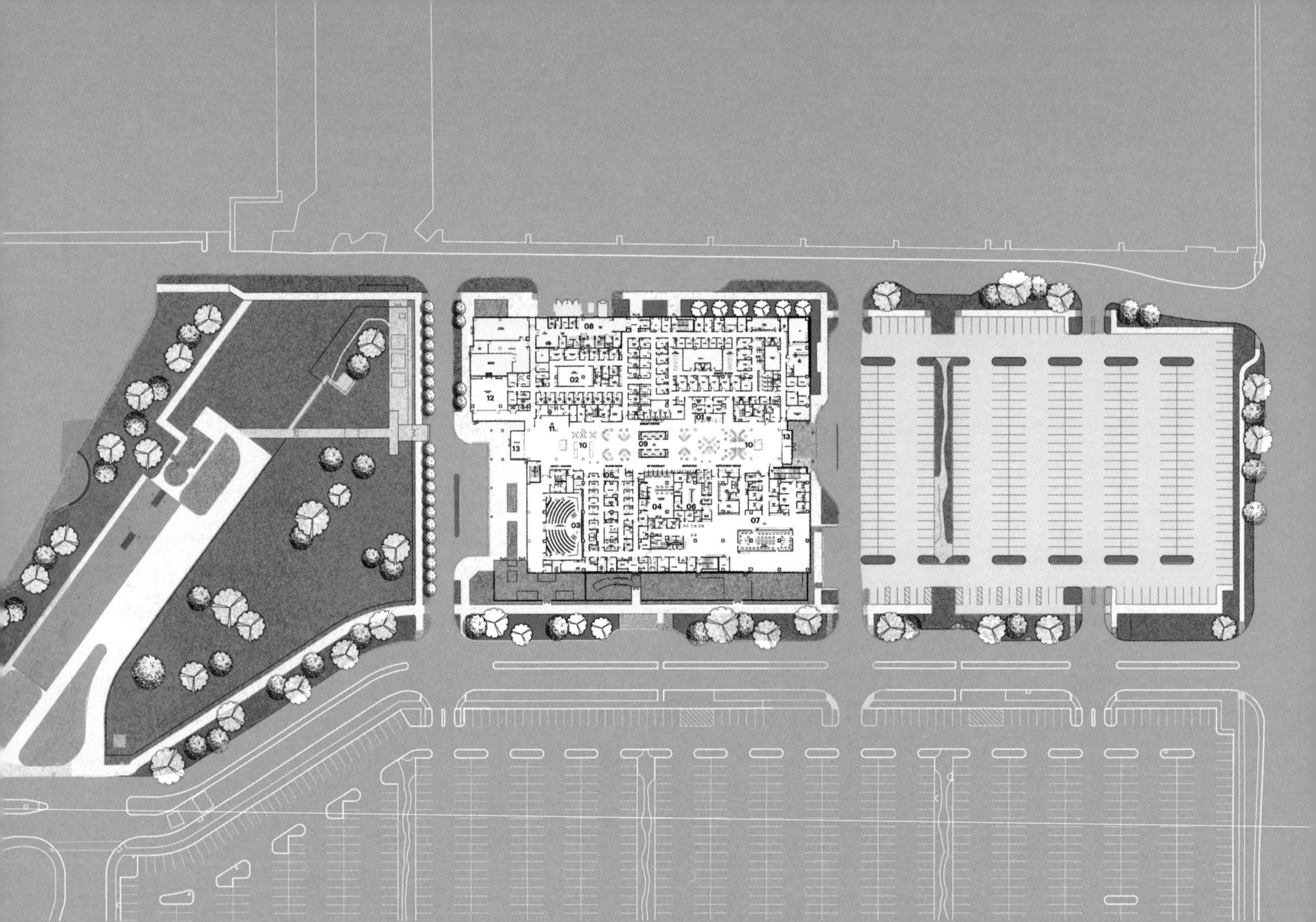

brain power and yellow trace paper. We spent lots of joint sessions working on flows of people and things and combined them, tested them, presented them, and amended them."

The modular clinic units contained in the outpatient center serve each specialty and facilitate easy flow between them. It allows for daily operational changes and future adjustments in health care management. The layout prioritizes accessibility, with high-traffic areas like intake and visitor spaces on the ground level and clinics spread across six floors, including the prominent Moody Center for Breast Health. The Center features inviting reception areas, a retail pharmacy, a coffee bar, and a rehabilitation garden, making it a premier destination for patient and staff well-being.

HKS looked at its larger portfolio to identify similar modular solutions for other healthcare clients and applied its knowledge of those situations to Parkland.

"Knowing that standardization offers efficiency and flexibility—and seeing it ripple across healthcare—helped us. We created something unique to Parkland, but it's based on a bigger trend in the healthcare industry," says Sheila Ruder, a Regional Practice Leader for Health and a principal at HKS. "A lot of it had to do with pulling together things we learned on previous projects—consolidating clinics into modules that provide flexibility, level-loading the clinics so there can be overflow during times of overutilization, or providing more clinical opportunity in less clinical space."

In the end, HKS's modular approach improved operating efficiency by twenty percent and improved the building's environmental standing by using materials and systems that reduce embodied carbon and water usage while maintaining high indoor air quality. The Center achieved LEED Gold Certification by the U.S. Green Building Council.

Hospitals like Parkland contribute to the larger economic and social health of their cities and counties. For the Moody Outpatient Center, forty-five percent of architecture and engineering contracts were awarded to Minority and Women-Owned Business Enterprises in Texas. Significantly, ninety-three percent of all contracts were awarded to Dallas County businesses.

N. CARROLLTON
DART
5:19 PM
138
DART

ACCESS TO CARE FOR ALL: Parkland Health's patient population often faces difficulties accessing health services and may be hesitant to seek care. To address this challenge, the Parkland Outpatient Clinic is located near Dallas Area Rapid Transit stations and the design emphasizes easy wayfinding and a calming atmosphere. Patients, visitors, and staff are welcomed to the Center via a landscaped park that replaced former parking lots and industrial lots. With its shaded seating areas and walking paths, the park encourages community members to engage with nature and view the campus as a destination rather than solely a place for medical treatment.

INFUSING HISTORY AND CULTURE: HKS' design for the mixed-use development at Vanke Hangzhou Waterfront explores the essence of traditional Chinese culture and melds it with contemporary design. Inspired by a Song Dynasty painting, it is composed with vibrancy, moments of pause, and a sensitive human scale approach.

The socioeconomic health of a community is often easy to perceive, but it's defined by a series of related dimensions that HKS evaluates to find design solutions for the communities it serves–including, in 2022, the comprehensive planning for the Vanke Hangzhou Waterfront in China's Zhejiang province. For a project like this one, says Bin Cao, Managing Director of East Asia, and a partner at HKS, the team had to think "in four dimensions, not just three," to unify two different residential programs and two sides of a city in the long run, befitting the status of this provincial capital city as an economic powerhouse.

The first residential program–or you could say the pretext for the entire project–was to create an athletes' village for the 2023 Asian Games. Hangzhou secured hosting duties–competing against other provincial capitals–on the strength of its waterfront along the Qiantang River, which winds nearly 400 miles to the sea and has been celebrated for centuries in poetry and painting. Today, the Qiantang River is a commercial artery that, like the Mississippi or Ohio Rivers, is defined as much by its economic importance as it is by its mythic status and vital ecology. In the past twenty years, cities like Hangzhou have

ELEGANT RESILIENCE STRATEGIES: Waterfront resilience—especially as it pertains to flooding—often includes green spaces that are intended to take on sudden overflows, as well as native plantings that are intended to take on routine drainage such as bioswales. The Vanke Hangzhou Waterfront integrates environmental sustainability with urban development using natural landscaping and innovative engineering to manage flood risks. As rainwater recharges the river, HKS has created a layering effect in its landscape that absorbs, deflects, or otherwise manages expected (or unexpected) water courses.

PLANNING FOR THE FUTURE: Adaptive reuse of athletes' villages promotes sustainability by repurposing existing structures and revitalizing urban spaces. At the Vanke Hangzhou Waterfront development, HKS transformed what began as temporary facilities into lasting assets for local residents, families, and workers. Adaptive reuse is more than a new lease on life for existing structures, it's a new lease on life for entire communities.

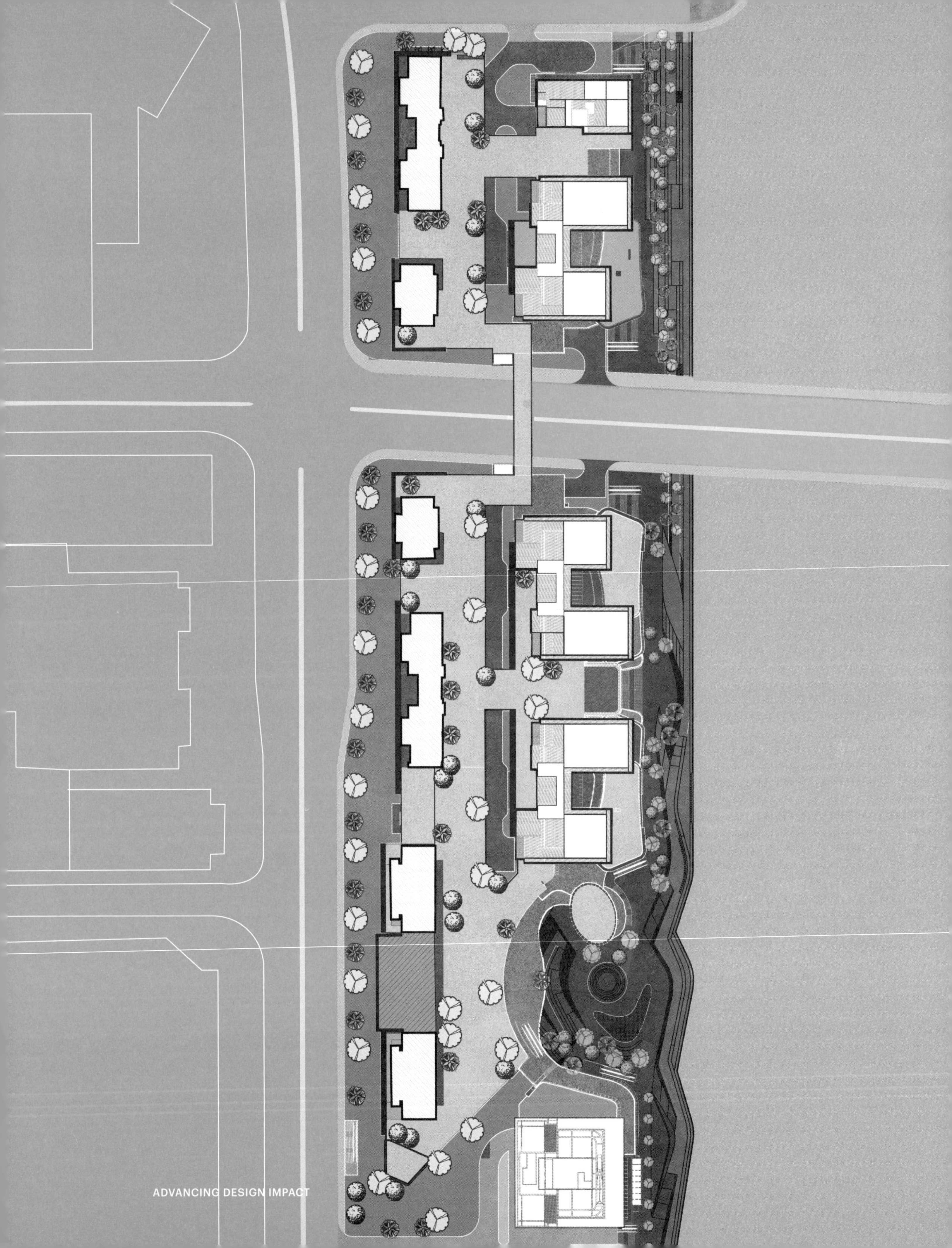

pursued waterfront economic development to revitalize underutilized spaces, enhancing tourism and recreation, as well as to attract businesses and investment—literally boosting local economies. There are biophilic advantages to spending time near water, too, improving the overall quality of life of those who live, work, or play nearby, not to mention the fact that waterfront development—along the Qiantang River or elsewhere—improves environmental resilience.

Athletes' villages, whether for the Asian Games or the international Olympics, are typically converted after their initial purpose, and they present unique challenges for architects such as balancing the temporary needs of thousands of athletes and the permanent needs of thousands more people who might raise their families there. For Hangzhou's Asian Games, HKS designed units to shelter 12,000 competitors from forty-five countries that were eventually converted to market-rate homes on a brownfield site. The firm's Shanghai team members also had the additional challenge of creating an entire district that had to transition smoothly from short-term housing to long-term, mixed commercial and residential uses.

As the anchor for a brand-new central business district, this project doesn't just set the stage for Hangzhou's next chapter. It is the stage and a "stage in the round," at that. The Vanke Hangzhou residential project is designed to have two fronts facing the Qinglong River and facing the southeast quadrants of the city. The design features eleven towers arranged around open spaces and recreational facilities—vestiges of the 2023 Asian Games. At the center of the development is a sunken water court, offering the sort of tranquility that anyone living in a city of ten million people will tell you is appreciated.

The towers themselves are uniquely shaped but share a cohesive design language that adds rhythm to the area—something you can perceive clearly along the

ECONOMIC OPPORTUNITY: The development brings an entirely new cultural and business district to Hangzhou. It includes destinations for leisure, shopping, and dining for local residents, and offices have attracted top global technology and commerce companies.

Qiantang River frontage. White, aluminum panels atop stone parapets create visual interest and create a calling card for a project that has put Hangzhou back on the map. More importantly, it has created a backdrop for the rhythms of everyday life.

"We see a lot of families and kids who are attracted to the waterfront space–and it's a lot of fun for them. People come here and spend time," says Cao. "The city is happy because it got a new landmark, and the people who live there are happy, too, so I think we feel it's a success."

Successful designers are able to help transform communities through positive outcomes and offer physical evidence of advancing design impact for all of us. HKS prioritizes people in its projects, creating spaces that foster interaction and inclusivity, ultimately enhancing well-being.

From developing the first football stadium in Los Angeles in nearly a hundred years to creating a community-focused outpatient center in Dallas, and revitalizing a riverfront district in Hangzhou, HKS collaborates with top professionals to deliver designs that inspire, engage, and enrich the fabric of cities and neighborhoods around the world.

But these three examples are just a taste of how HKS' enriching designs contribute to dynamic and thriving civic life. With each passing year, the firm's diverse, global design teams push themselves to connect more with people they design for and leverage their skills and talents to generate ideas for places that are meaningful and well-loved.

Each project reflects a commitment to integrating technology, ecology, and local needs, demonstrating the profound impact thoughtful, beautiful design can have on society.

END NOTES

1. Reyner Banham, *Los Angeles: The Architecture of Four Ecologies*, Penguin Press, 1971.

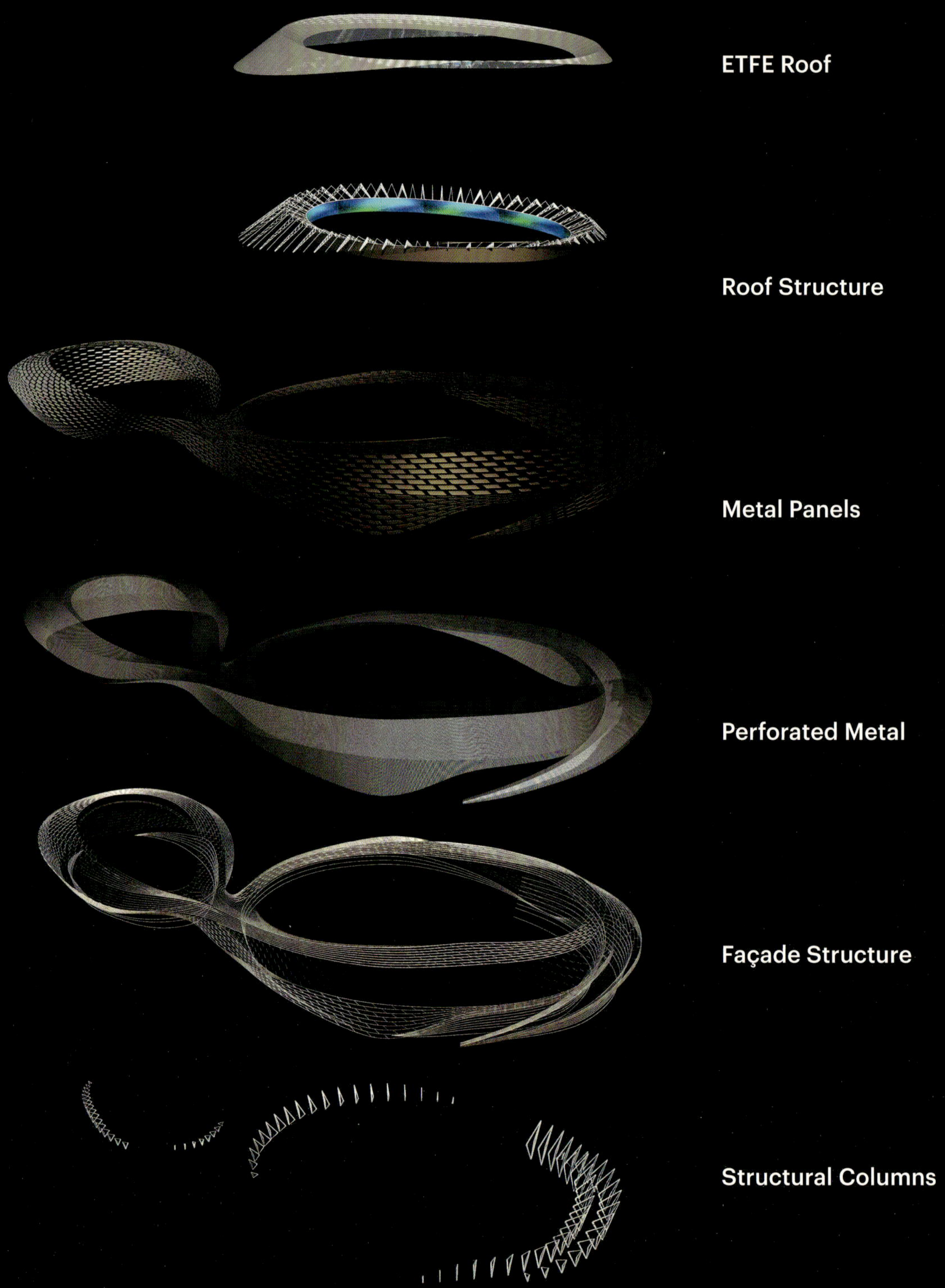
ETFE Roof
Roof Structure
Metal Panels
Perforated Metal
Façade Structure
Structural Columns

A STRUCTURAL SPECTACLE: Chengdu Phoenix Hill Sports Park is a community anchor designed for the highest-grade professional competitions and exciting community experiences. Circular forms connect the stadium and arena, and the stadium's roof is comprised of the country's first open cable dome structure with a massive single-layer cable system and translucent ethylene tetrafluoroethylene (ETFE) membrane structure that shields spectators from the elements and allows natural light to flow inside.

BUILDING CONNECTIONS: HALL Arts Residences are part of a mixed-use development located in the heart of the Dallas Arts District. The development also includes HALL Arts Hotel, commercial and retail establishments, and community amenities such as the Texas Sculpture Walk, which bridges the Arts District with the Central Business District and tells the story of Dallas through public art.

usbankstadium

U.S. BANK STADIUM

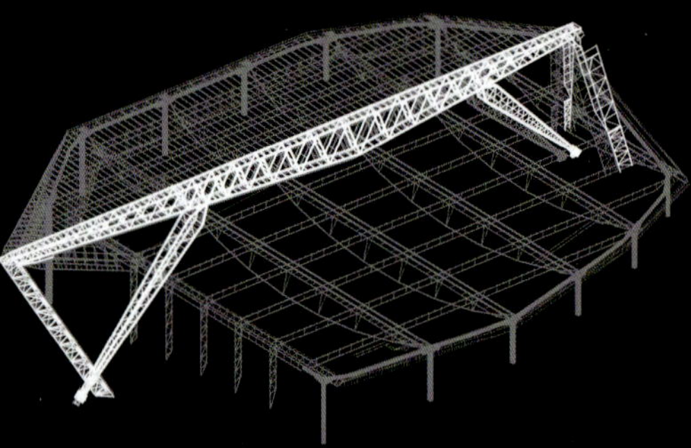

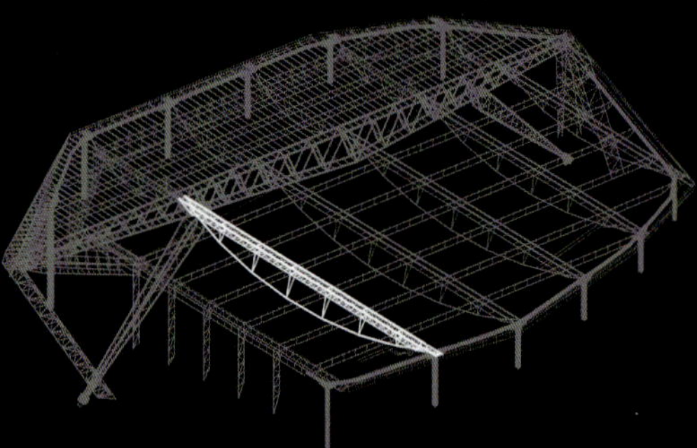

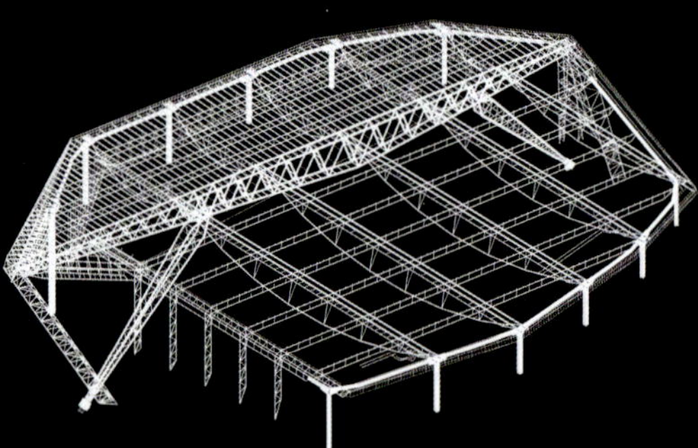

usbankstadium
VIKINGS

SITE-SPECIFIC DESIGN: U. S. Bank Stadium's roof is the lynchpin of the venue's custom, Minnesota Vikings-inspired design. Since a retractable roof wasn't the right solution for cold and snow-stricken Minneapolis, the HKS team and collaborators developed the enclosed roof to be asymmetrical with a single longitudinal beam/super truss. Its steep pitch allows heavy snow loads to slide into containment basins and the transparent ETFE material allows daylight to flood in so fans feel like they are as close to being outside as possible without having to weather the elements.

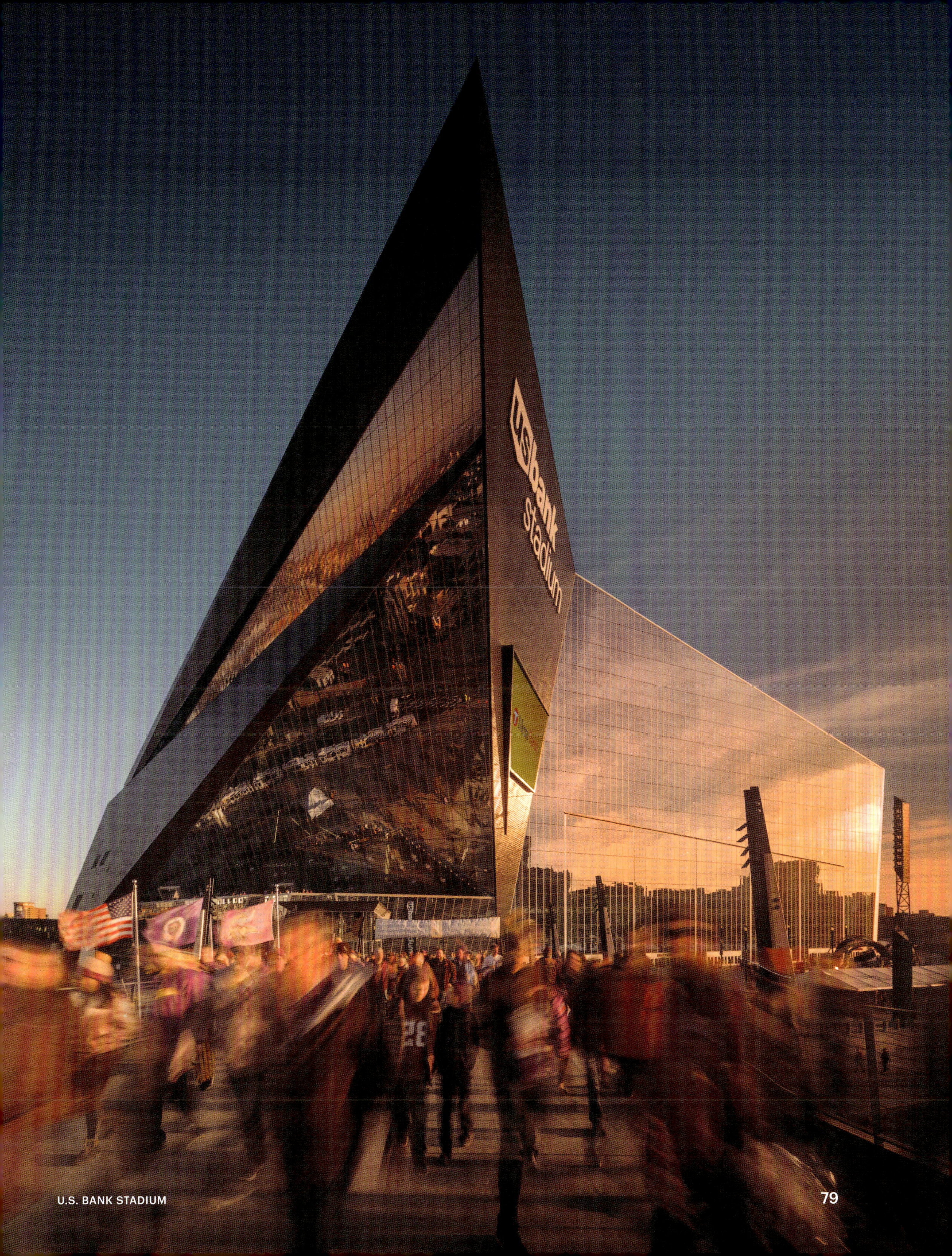
usbank
stadium

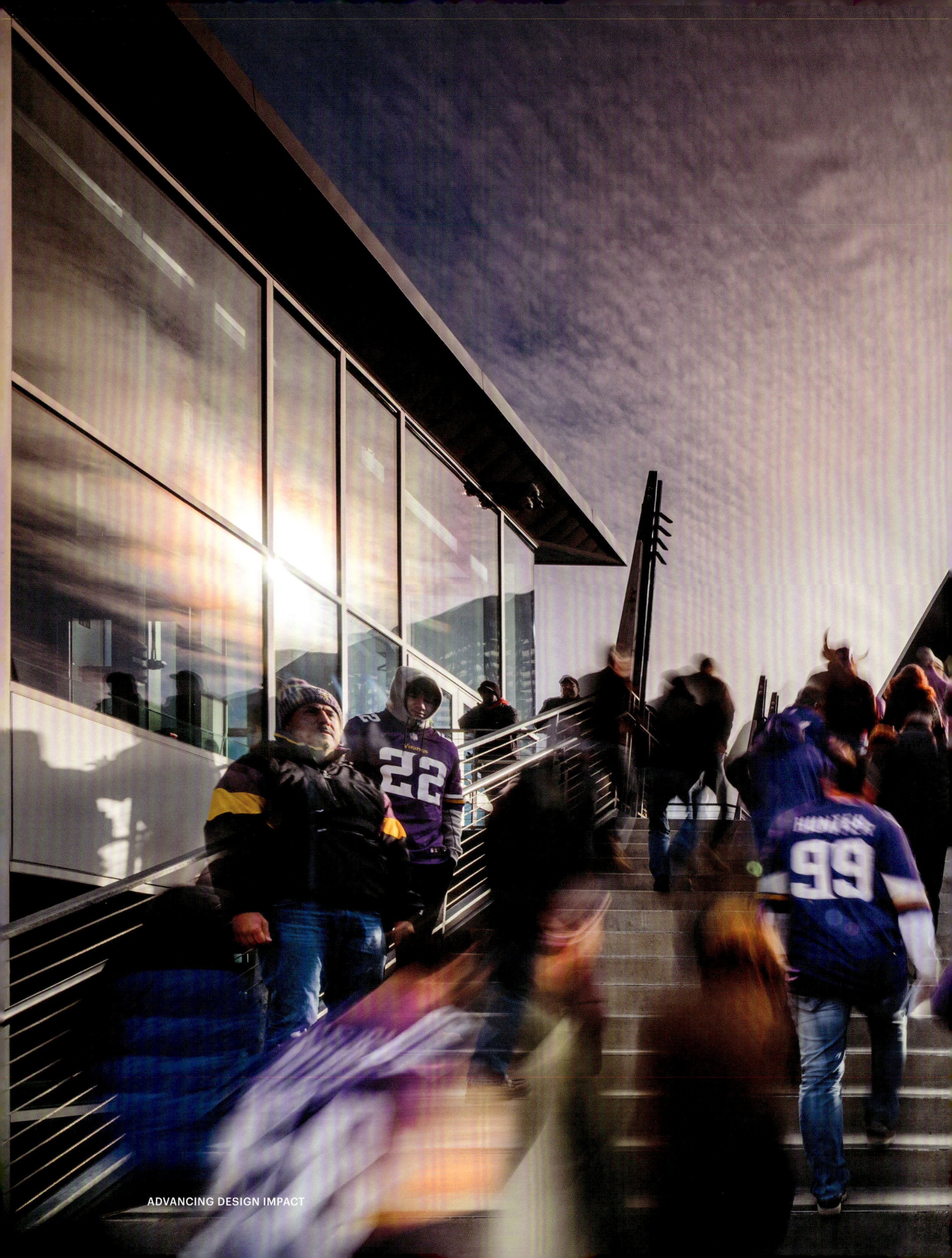
VIKINGS
22
99

us bank
stadium

SECTIONS 301 - 305
ENTRY 10 ELEVATORS
& STAIRS
SECTIONS 306 & 307

MG
NATION

MGM

MGM

1

INNOVATION ON THE PRAIRIE: The Dakota State University Applied Research Lab is designed as a luminous structure that hovers above the prairie and blends seamlessly with the natural landscape. The building plans feature serrated façades that introduce daylight without compromising security, creating an environment that is both inviting and protective.

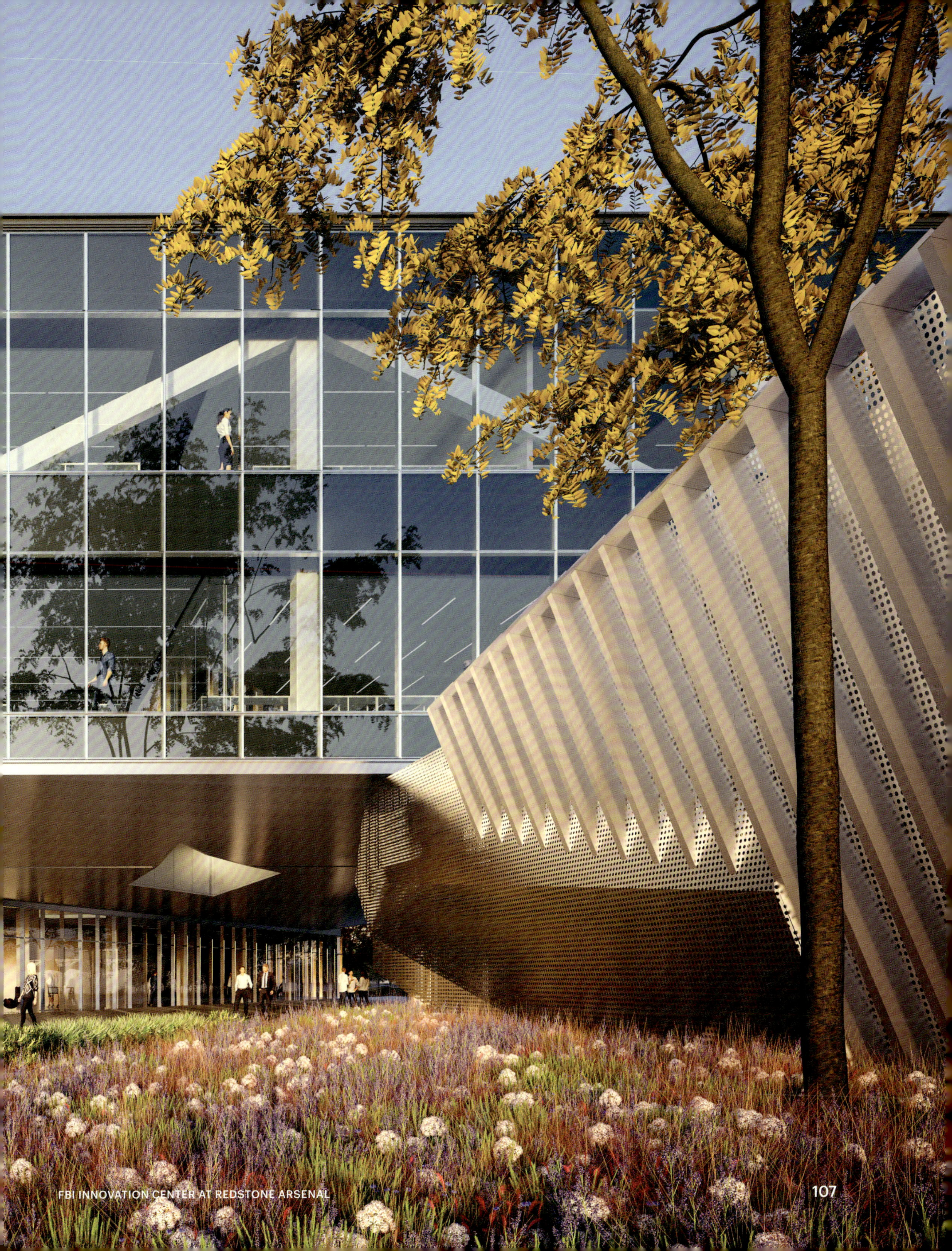

Fairmont

CHINATI

INVITING PEOPLE IN: Edison House, a social club in Salt Lake City, features locally manufactured brick that references the club's historic Warehouse District location. In contrast, the building's metal panels embody a contemporary expression that connects with the city's nearby downtown Central Business District. A primary façade features perforated and bi-folding screens as well as lift-and-slide doors that flex to support programming needs and invite community members in, reflecting the club's ethos of inclusivity.

A KINETIC FAÇADE: Created through custom design and fabrication with project partners, Edison House's façade includes screens made of aluminum tube frames that are lightweight enough to move manually and aid the thermal comfort throughout the building. The operable screens can be adjusted individually, meaning there is often a dynamic interplay of exterior elements that mirrors the vibrant activities within the building.

2000 ROSS AND JW MARRIOTT DALLAS ARTS DISTRICT

COMMUNITY CATALYST: HKS designed two buildings, layered on top of one another, that have enhanced the public realm in the Dallas Arts District. 2000 Ross features fritted glass that conceals the building's function as a parking garage along a major corridor and a mix of street-level retail uses that provide much-needed amenities. The JW Marriot Arts District, which sits atop 2000 Ross, creates energy and activity suited to the dynamic surrounding neighborhood with views of the Dallas skyline and public spaces adorned with sculptural elements and thought-provoking artwork.

Image Credits

SoFi Stadium and Hollywood Park
Photography: © Jason O'Rear (12–13); © Nic Lehoux (16–17, 22, 24–25); © Bruce Damonte (19–21); © HKS, Inc. (23)

Moody Outpatient Center at Parkland Hospital
Photography: © Tom Harris (26–29, 31 top, 32–35, 37–39); © HKS, Inc., Daryl Shields (30, 31 bottom)

Vanke Hangzhou Waterfront
Photography: © Shanghai Yizhu Photography Studio, Terrance Zhang (40–41,44–45, 49–50); © WangJiaDi (42–43, 46 top, 47, 51); © Bing Lu (46 bottom)

Chengdu Phoenix Hill Sports Park
Photography: © Chengdu Arch-Exist Photography Co., Ltd. (53–59, 65); © Z/S Studio (63); © JC Photography (60–61, 64)

HALL Arts Residences
Photography: © Alex Fradkin Photography (66–69)

U.S. Bank Stadium
Photography: © Mark Goodman Photography (70–71); © Corey Gaffer (72); © Aker Imaging (74–77); © Nic Lehoux (73, 78–79, 80–81)

YouTube Theater
Photography: © Bruce Damonte (82–83)

MGM National Harbor
Photography: © Alex Fradkin Photography (84–89, 92–95); © Prakash Patel (90–91)

Bell Textron Advanced Vertical Lift Business Center
Photography: © Evan Thomas @ Studio Thomas Photography (96–99)

Dakota State University Applied Research Lab
Renderings: © HKS, Inc. (100–105)

FBI Innovation Center at Redstone Arsenal
Rendering: © HKS, Inc. (106–107)

W Bellevue Hotel and Residences
Design: ROAM Interior Design
Photography: © Garrett Rowland Photography (108–111)

Fairmont Taghazout Bay
Photography: © Javier Callejas (112–115)

Hotel Saint George
Design: ROAM Interior Design
Photography: © Casey Dunn (116–119)

Edison House
Photography: © Garrett Rowland Photography (120–123)

2000 Ross and JW Marriott Dallas Arts District
Photography: © Alex Fradkin Photography (124–125, 128); © HKS, Inc., Daryl Shields (126–127)

DRIVING INNOVATION THROUGH INQUIRY

Some people believe the quality of any answer depends on the quality of the original question. That's one of the central tenets of design research, which comes in lots of varieties on the spectrum between science and art. Outcome-driven design is research-driven design, and it's a vital pursuit for HKS, which marshals data and real-world insights to inform design decisions, ensuring user experience and sustainability are optimized.

By fostering a culture of continuous improvement, HKS refines its design methodologies. Whether for a university campus, a healthcare non-profit's headquarters, or a workplace café, HKS uses tools of investigation to optimize and validate design decisions. They also gather feedback in a number of ways, including post-occupancy evaluations to measure how spaces function after they are built. This feedback informs future designs, enhancing patient, student, or worker outcomes such as improved physical and mental health and increased operational efficiency.

Additionally, the firm regularly engages with clients and stakeholders to understand their evolving needs, allowing for innovative solutions that respond to changing contexts. HKS' commitment to sustainability also drives continuous improvement, with the firm actively tracking energy performance data from its buildings. This informs future projects and helps set new benchmarks in sustainable architecture, ultimately leading to better designs that benefit both people and the environment.

IMPROVING HEALTH OF PEOPLE AND PLANET: Previously a surface parking lot, North Torrey Pines Living and Learning Community at UC San Diego was the largest construction project in the University's history at the time it was constructed. It includes three residence halls, two academic buildings, classrooms, administration offices, underground parking and public amenities amounting to 1,633,188 square feet of total building area. The design-build project team, led by HKS, employed evidence-based design strategies to encourage healthy habits, cultivate social connections, and minimize environmental impact on the sensitive coastal site.

At the core of outcome-driven design is the belief that research has the power to transform architectural projects, yielding benefits for the communities they serve.

Torrey Pines in La Jolla is one such community. It is named for its hearty evergreens, some hundreds of years old, whose rough-hewn trunks burst skyward in a riot of needles, some as long as eight inches. The pines define this enclave of laboratories, resorts, residential communities, as well as a University of California San Diego campus designed by HKS, completed in 2021, and standing in careful balance with the intertidal and desert ecosystems along this coastal bluff. HKS drew together the academic and residential needs of 2,000 students, faculty, and staff in a community with thermal comfort strategies that provide advantages in the face of our extreme climate futures. It's the largest living and learning community across the university's 10 campuses. It's also a beacon for students who, through their experiences there, connect stewardship of a fragile ecosystem to the resilient design solutions that tomorrow's campuses might employ.

By 2010, UC San Diego decided to expand campus facilities after realizing their projected student housing shortage was more dire than expected and set out to develop the North Torrey Pines Living and Learning Neighborhood (NTPLLN) with the added goal of helping the university achieve its carbon neutrality goal by 2025. HKS designers were tasked with creating a campus that not only addressed housing needs but also supported the health and well-being of its users. The firm led a design-build project team that included Clark Construction, Safdie Rabines Architects, and OJB Landscape Architecture, transforming a collection of small student cabins and a surface parking lot into a vibrant, multi-functional campus. The development includes three residence halls and two mixed-use academic buildings, resulting in a total building area of more than 1.6 million square feet.

"The biggest challenge with creating a campus like this is how you deal with scale and density," says Thom Greving, a former Regional Design Director for HKS' education practice and the design lead on the

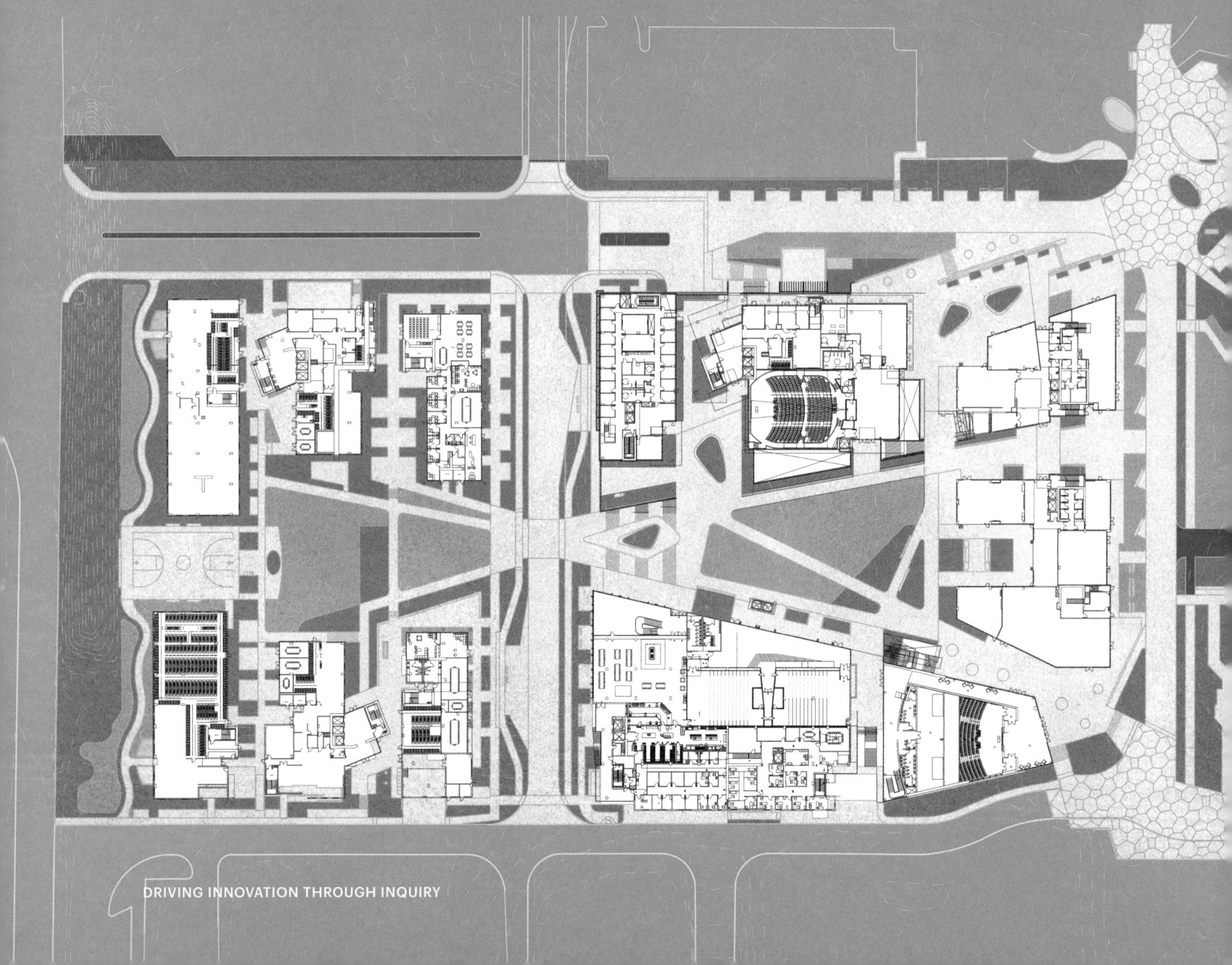

DESIGNED FOR CONNECTION AND GROWTH: NTPLLN is a mixed-use environment that fosters connections among students, staff, faculty and local community members with a diverse array of gathering areas, dining establishments and a market in addition to its residential and academic spaces. A Triple Bottom Line-Cost Benefit Analysis illuminated that the project will provide economic value of more than $600 million to the UC San Diego and La Jolla community in the years to come.

CREATIVITY AND COMMUNITY: One of the most popular and unique spaces at NTPLLN is the Craft Center, pictured above, which features a surfboard shaping shop and offers affordable art classes for members of both the UC San Diego and La Jolla communities.

project, "by taking a campus of cute little cabins for students–and then going from that to a full-blown neighborhood."

HKS also focused on another kind of scale that's often difficult to define: the well-being of a student population. In collaboration with the non-profit Center for Advanced Design Research and Evaluation (CADRE), HKS partnered with U.C. San Diego faculty and the Academy of Neuroscience for Architecture to launch a longitudinal study examining how built environments impact student health, well-being, social connection, and environmental health. The cross-disciplinary team compared students' experiences in their previous residential settings with those in new environments one year later, assessing changes in perceptions and behaviors. COVID-19 altered the researchers' methodology and forced the team to adapt to a hybrid model of in-person observations and online data-collection, yet the study proved successful and both pre- and post-move data led to firm conclusions about how design could improve well-being on the campus itself.

Greving says the team pursued what it calls a "restorative landscape" that could knit together complicated elements of a live/learn campus program with a robust natural ecosystem. Constrained on all four sides by other campus developments and four existing roads (including one named for the naturalist John Muir), HKS had to make every square foot count. "The spaces between buildings were designed to give students lots of opportunities to adapt and use those places so Torrey Pines can live up to its name as a functioning live/learn neighborhood," he says.

The design promotes physical activity and social interaction with features such as stairs, outdoor gathering spaces, and access to healthy food options. Connected pathways and bikeways that stitch this campus together with its neighborhood have also created a twenty-one-point bump in the site's walk-score, from forty-five percent in 2021 to sixty-six percent in 2022–making mobility less of a checklist amity and more of a way of life. Mobility is the centerpiece of the "point of decision-making" framework used by the design team led by HKS, which had one goal: make the healthy

RESEARCH-LED DESIGN: HKS, the Center for Advanced Design Research and Evaluation (CADRE) and UC San Diego pursued a longitudinal study to understand the impact of the built environment on the student experience. They assessed student behaviors related to social connection, learning, well-being, and space utilization as well as environmental stewardship in NTPLLN as compared to previous residential environments. The study revealed that upon moving to NTPPLN, students self-reported an 8.2 percent reduction in depression, a 12.85 percent increase in satisfaction with social spaces, and a 27.96 percent increase in satisfaction with residential spaces.

option the easy option for students. Whether they're hankering for a smoothie or trekking to class, students have optimized possibilities for physical activity and holistic well-being.

"For me, it's about sustainability and wellness. Tuning a piano is the same as fine-tuning a campus that embraces holistic design," says Tommy Zakrzewski, Director of Building Engineering Physics and a principal at HKS. "Tuning three strings and finding the right pitch for a note. That's what sustainability and wellness was like for us: creating a built environment that supports students so they may excel."

Despite the challenges posed by the COVID-19 pandemic, chief among them the mental health strain of isolation, students reported an 8.2 percent reduction in depression. This was a direct result of the HKS team's focus on connectivity as a foundation for health and well-being on campus–and conceived long before the pandemic swept through southern California.

"The students felt better connected during COVID because they had better visual lines of sight–and they saw activity around them at a time when everyone was so isolated," says Upali Nanda,Global Sector Director of Innovation and a partner and executive vice president at HKS. "UC San Diego doesn't have a campus green like other campuses, but Torrey Pines created that amenity."

NTPLLN exemplifies how a thoughtfully designed campus can address housing needs while promoting sustainability, well-being, and community engagement. That's the basis of its accolades from the American Institute of Architects' Committee on the Environment, which recognized it with a Top 10 award–the industry's best-known recognition for innovation, sustainability, and design excellence. NTPLLN incorporates energy-efficient design strategies, with over one-third of the building area un-airconditioned and all student bedrooms equipped with operable windows and advanced ventilation systems. The campus features the university's first micro-anaerobic digester, which produces renewable energy and organic fertilizer from food waste.

NTPLLN takes full advantage of San Diego's climate and its coastal location. The design includes native and drought-tolerant plants, which create habitats for wildlife and contribute to biophilic benefits. Green spaces and roof terraces enhance the connection to nature, while water-efficient landscaping and rainwater filtration systems address local drought conditions and conserve resources. As a result, it's the largest LEED Platinum higher education project in California, with an eighty-one percent reduction in energy use intensity (otherwise known as EUI) and a forty percent combined increase in student satisfaction for social and residential spaces.

"Activation is an outcome of a well-designed landscape and well-built environment. That's the proof. The behaviors you see–like students relaxing and connecting with each other? Also proof," says Nanda. "You can layer all the simulations onto the site that you like, but we have the behavior mapping to show that those simulations worked–and our intentions for scale and site were proven."

In the interests of transparency, HKS has made the project's award-winning design research publicly available online as a contribution to other evidence-based design researchers. But, the campus offers another kind of contribution that's a little closer to home and, at the same time, broader in its impact to other populations in the San Diego area. By offering 2,048 beds at below-market rates, NTPLLN provides affordable housing in a high-cost region, with obvious economic and social benefits for students, positively benefiting the local housing market and, in turn, benefitting staff, faculty, and local residents.

When the design team conducted a Triple Bottom Line-Cost Benefit Analysis, highlighting the potential for long-term economic growth and value generation for both the university and the community, it was clear this was more than a new campus for students. This was a new mixed-use engine for the local economy, generating an estimated $611 million in value for the students, the school and its staff, and the larger La Jolla community.

TRUE HIGH-PERFORMANCE: Designed for energy performance, NTPLLN relies on passive strategies and high-efficiency systems. More than one third of the total building area is unconditioned and every student bedroom has operable windows, leading to an eighty-one percent reduction of Energy Use Intensity (EUI). Each of the buildings—which all achieved LEED Platinum Certification—feature connected indoor and outdoor spaces that make the most of San Diego's climate and NTPLLN's site on the Pacific Coast.

A NEXUS FOR CONNECTION: The Alcon Novartis café building sits in the center of the medical research campus on top of a knoll, a well-connected location at the nexus of multiple pathways. Situated between different programmatic campus functions, the café, which features an open kitchen and open seating, acts as a common meeting ground where spontaneous interactions and moments of reflection by staff and researchers are made possible.

It's easy (and often enjoyable) to think about architecture and design projects as stand-alone objects that are beautifully crafted and even sculptural, and to compare them to other buildings from different times and places. It's harder and, arguably, just as important, to consider how projects are deeply tied to their streets, neighborhoods, cities, and regions—to reflect on their implications for their times and places. Architecture, in this sense, matters to people at lots of different scales or, "from a spoon to the city," to quote the Italian architect Ernesto Rogers, when he expressed his desire to make design a unifying force in our lives.

Connectivity, the degree to which spaces and places encourage and support people getting together and easily moving around, is something HKS excelled at creating for one of its rarer project types: a café for the 500 scientific researchers and administrative staff who work at the Alcon research facility in Fort Worth, Texas, which was commissioned by Alcon's then-owner, Novartis. HKS designed the space to be multipurpose with 270 degrees of dining and meeting areas encircling the building's interior, featuring various seating arrangements to accommodate groups of different sizes.

Novartis envisioned a centralized dining amenity for its employees who, as a circumstance of their work, are usually siloed. Bringing them together to challenge the silos usually associated with corporate campuses or bringing them together simply for a meal. Bringing them together also meant giving them something to enjoy once they got there, evident in the space's floor-to-ceiling views of a lush landscape. But, how does all that glass work in the Texas sun?

The HKS team conducted extensive daylight analysis for the roof of the café and its overhang so people could have comfortable eating space with southern exposure all year long. They analyzed the roof geometry so the space could offer unfettered views of the surrounding landscape, which led to the use of large expanses of glass in the design. The distinctive,

COMPUTATION AND INNOVATION: By incorporating parametric and building energy modeling early in the process, the HKS team fine-tuned the design for high performance in local North Texas climate. Using a genetic solver, a computational tool with algorithms inspired by biological evolution, the team defined the roof form and overhang distances on the south side of the building to guarantee maximum shading during the summer months and extend the hours of comfort along the building's periphery. The open day-lit interior environment minimizes direct solar gain and glare, with a southern exterior dining area that remains shaded during café hours and a northside dining experience with controlled and filtered natural light. These efforts led to reduced energy consumption and an increased number of hours that the spaces can be comfortably used, enhancing how the design supports people coming together to socialize and connect.

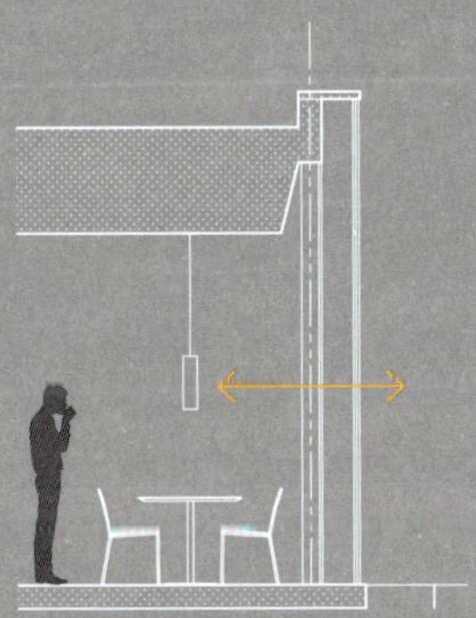

Glass Fin

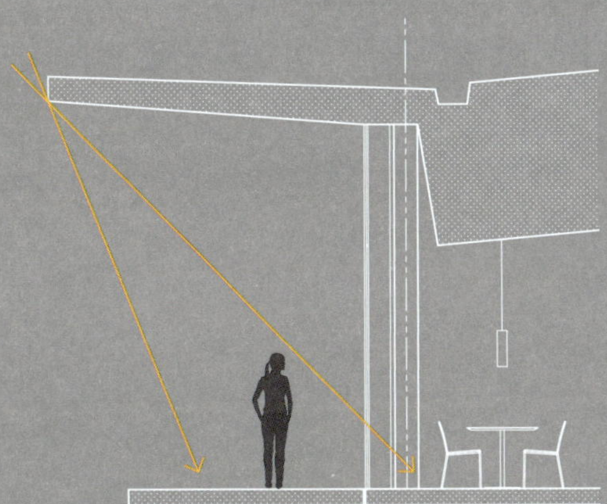

Curtain Wall

undulating roofline bends to meet the needs of specific orientations that maximize thermal comfort under the harshest of sun conditions.

Beneath the roof, which provides ample natural light, thin columns allow for unobstructed views and a seamless connection between indoor and outdoor spaces. This design not only emphasizes transparency and openness but also reflects the innovative spirit of the clients' research enterprise, which aligns with their commitment to a forward-thinking, employee-centered work environment. Such spareness, though, means that details count more than anything–including the seams where soffit meets roof and column. "The columns are simply painted with a fire-rated paint and that helps preserve their thinness to keep the view outside. The wood soffit brings warmth to the project, and the sloping of the roof offers visual diversity," says Jon Bailey, a Practice Design Director for HKS' Laboratory for INtensive Exploration (LINE), "and it all comes together for people in a seamless way–even if those seams were half the battle."

With all that natural light, the next question is how to harness it without creating uncomfortable hot spots or untenable glare. HKS implemented innovative sun-shading techniques in the Alcon Novartis project to enhance energy efficiency and occupant comfort through a combination of vertical fins and cantilevered overhangs that effectively block direct sunlight while allowing natural light to permeate the interiors. These vertical fins are strategically placed to mitigate glare and heat gain, particularly during peak sun hours, reducing reliance on artificial lighting and HVAC systems.

Additionally, the roof's overhangs create shaded outdoor areas that encourage social interaction and relaxation. This approach not only optimizes thermal performance but also aligns with the project's commitment to sustainability. By integrating these sun-shading elements, HKS architects created a space that balances light, shade, and views, fostering a pleasant environment for employees while minimizing energy consumption. Overall, these techniques demonstrate HKS' dedication to thoughtful, evidence-based design that prioritizes user experience and environmental responsibility.

Connectivity remained the chief strategy for the design team, who aimed to make the new 21,000-square-foot space a central hub for researchers in medical technology and the administrators who support the mission. This collaborative environment is essential–as a counterpoint to siloed, heads-down work, but also as an opportunity for interdisciplinary interactions to thrive. The design fosters spontaneous conversations and collaboration between scientists, technicians, and researchers, enhancing the synergy between administration and research areas on the campus.

BLENDING ARCHITECTURE AND LANDSCAPE: The Alcon Novartis café was designed with careful consideration of its natural surroundings. With preserved southern live oak trees and a focal water feature running the campus, the project minimized environmental impact and led to a building that seamlessly blends with the landscape.

PROMEDICA
PROMEDICA

FIFTH THIRD BANK

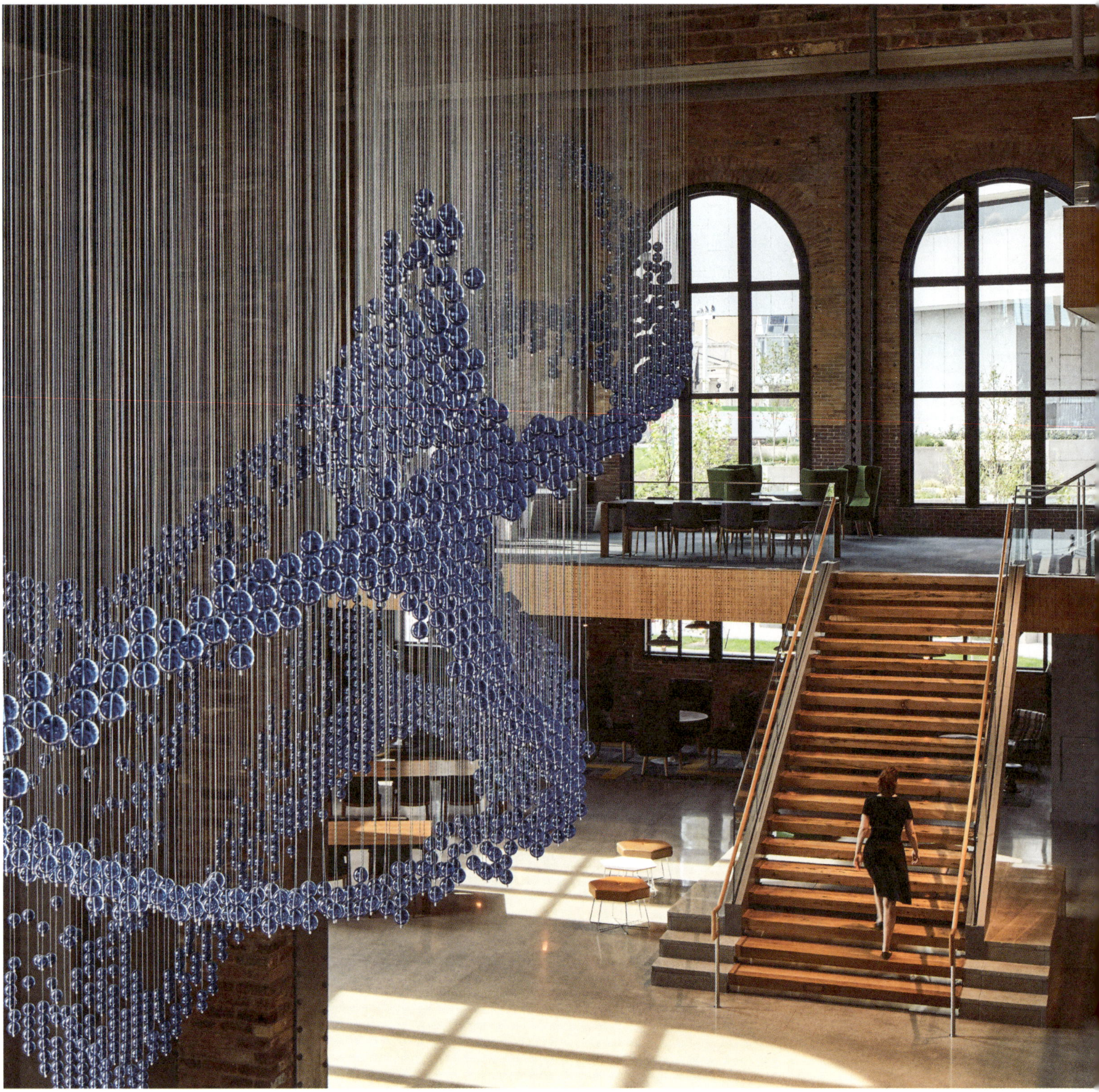

BRIDGING THE PAST AND FUTURE: ProMedica Headquarters is an adaptive reuse of an historic steam plant and a Brutalist junction building next to Promenade Park on Toledo's Maumee River. The design celebrates the site's heritage and energizes the waterfront with new life. The steam plant building's large machine rooms were transformed into open office space with amenities, and 100 percent of the building's brick was reused in the construction. A life cycle analysis of the project revealed that by repurposing existing buildings and materials for the project, the HKS team reduced embodied carbon by seventy percent, or more than 1600 metric tons, meaning the project had significantly lower environmental impact than new construction would have.

When the nonprofit healthcare organization ProMedica called longtime research and design partner HKS to reimagine its corporate headquarters in Toledo, Ohio, the firm accepted knowing it would have to focus on designing for connectivity in new ways. Unlike the integrated hospitals and clinics HKS had designed for ProMedica previously, this time, connections would be created between a steam plant from 1897 and an electrical junction building from 1965, and among nearly 1,500 employees. That's not counting the thousands of employees that have made ProMedica a regional powerhouse with twelve hospitals that treat nearly five million patients each year.

HKS's work for ProMedica launched the company's multi-year effort to relocate the full administrative team downtown, focusing on a nimble workplace and enabling quick department relocations while accommodating the "hot-desking" model that many hybrid companies have come to rely on. HKS considered how new spaces could foster employee investment at a deeper level than job descriptions and goal attainment, which they also saw as a talent acquisition strategy. To guide design decisions, ProMedica launched an employee engagement initiative, nominating ambassadors who were part of the earliest schematic design phases at HKS, whose designers sought out guidance and feedback from the ambassadors on a continual basis. Initial engagement included workshops to understand daily experiences and preferences. This approach helped identify concerns about the current workspaces and eased fears related to the transition, ensuring broader employee involvement in the design process.

In consolidating various offices to create a ProMedica campus along the banks of the Maumee River, HKS adapted the site's existing structures and built two new structures to meet the needs of its on-site workers. The campus is also located in an

economically distressed area of Ohio, with a poverty rate of forty-five percent and an unemployment rate of fourteen percent–making the project an important job generator and, for its riverside site, a vital opportunity to create a semi-public park space.

"What made this project exciting is it provided the chance to get to know Toledo better and discover what a waterfront community catalyst could be–as an economic force and as a steward," says Anthony Montalto, Chief Design Officer and a partner at HKS. "The site, itself–for me–it had a historical component and a symbolic one. We had to do something that was future-focused and complementary to the past."

ProMedica's site featured a steam plant designed by Daniel Burnham, the famed American architect who designed, among other things, New York's Flatiron Building and Chicago's urban plan (and whose firm, D.H. Burnham and Co., was the largest architecture office in the world at the time of his death). Completed in 1897, the steam plant had been in decline structurally for many years by the time HKS stepped in–a hulking shell on the Maumee, destined for the wrecking ball. ProMedica's site also featured a nearby electrical junction house designed and completed in the 1960s in the Brutalist style. Both buildings had seen better days, but the HKS design team knew that if it was going to create something that was both familiar and future-facing for ProMedica, both buildings must be part of its new scheme.

"Architecture is always a timeline of culture connected by nature and humanity," says Montalto, "and we really feel like that comes out here–in the new construction and in the structures we adapted."

Adapting an existing building is not without surprises. Lisa Adams, Director of Citizen HKS, a Sustainable Design Leader for Interiors and principal at HKS, says she would get a constant stream of calls during the construction phase of the project about a

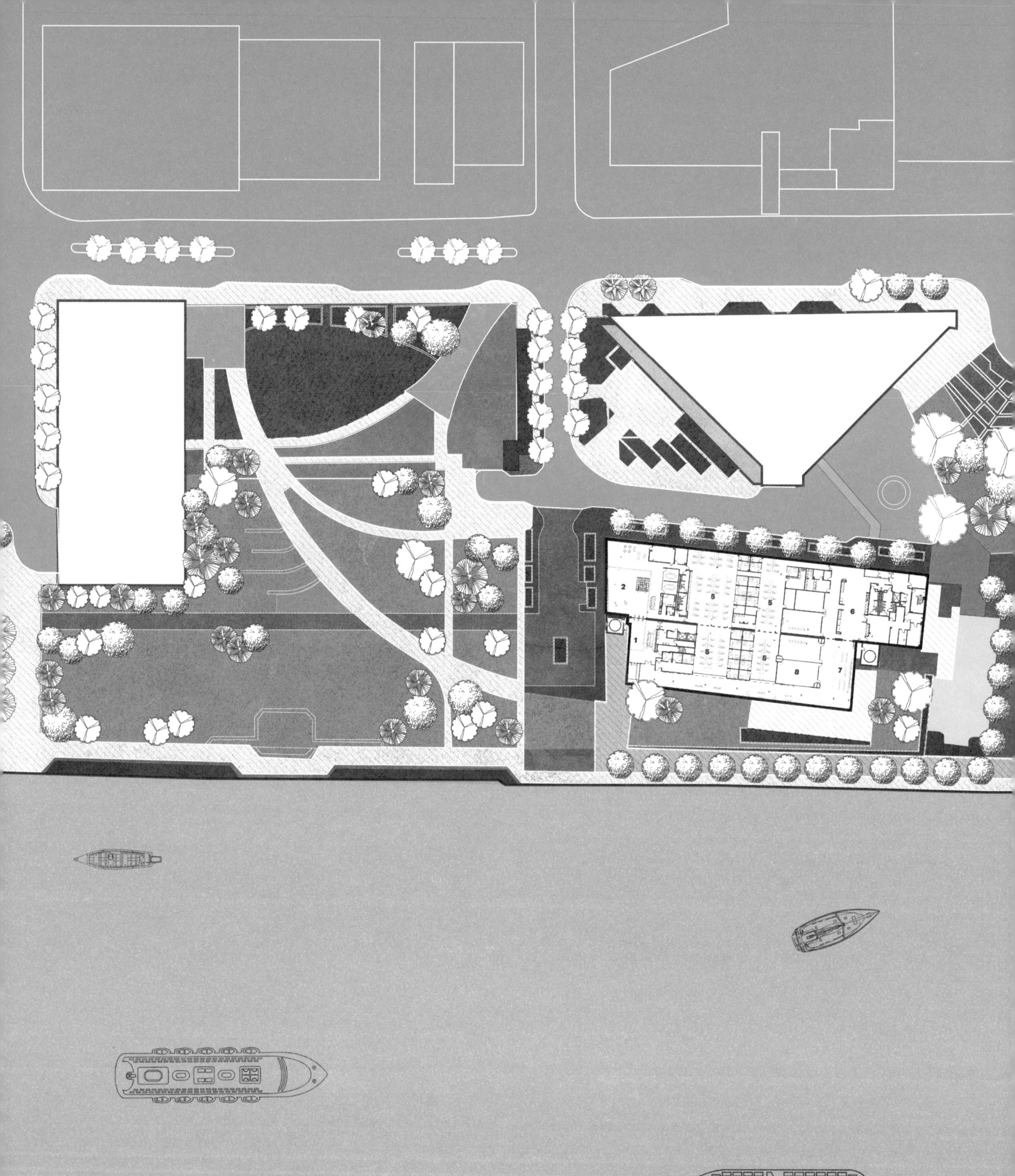
2
5
5
6
1
5
5
8
7

newly discovered trap door. "We couldn't have anticipated these discoveries, so we made those elements part of the design," she says, "and, if there were things we couldn't incorporate into the renovation, we used them outside."

Adapting an existing workforce to a centralized headquarters is also not without its challenges. Adams, Montalto, and the team worked directly with hundreds of employees who enjoyed reporting to satellite offices to both entice them with a new working model and create a new language of spaces. "We wanted to create more flexibility for them," Adams says," and quite literally break down walls and barriers."

That meant creating a set of modules for working teams, who could enjoy semi-public and semi-private spaces spread out over a variety of interiors–from the steam plant's dramatic new staircase and cavernous new meet-up spot, to more conventional cubicles for heads-down work. That also meant giving people lots of reasons to stay active during the day–befitting a health and wellness nonprofit–including the 5,500 square-foot YMCA on the building's lower level and dining choices on the ground floor.

Connections to nature were also important tactics for the design team to eliminate the barriers that have typically defined office life. It's not uncommon for ProMedica teams to have impromptu meetings on the fourth-floor roof deck with panoramic views, and the cafeteria a few floors down opens directly onto the riverwalk. Every space in the newly constituted campus is suffused with light thanks to generous windows, certainly on the nineteenth century steam plant, but also throughout the rest of the campus.

Did the design team succeed in creating the kind of connectivity that this part of Toledo–and ProMedica–sorely needed? The proof is everywhere, from the CEO's own report back that, after the staff's first year there, the reduction in emails was notable. People seemed to prefer getting up and walking over to see their colleagues rather than grinding it out over a keyboard. The riverfront park, itself, also hosted eighteen events in its first year since ProMedica moved in–an unthinkable number a decade before–drawing-in residents and the other workers in this part of the city for a summer concert at the end of a busy week.

PUBLIC ART AND PUBLIC SPACE: A ring sculpture by the artists Kristine Rumman and Dane Turpening is located at ProMedica Headquarters. Called "Echo," it explores the relationship between historical and modern architecture, honoring Toledo's industrial history while embracing contemporary design that reflects cultural and technological advancements. The development surrounding ProMedica Headquarters is now a thriving public space where farmers markets and community festivals are held.

A SEAMLESS WORKPLACE: ProMedica Headquarters is a modern workplace that bridges old and new architecture as well as historic and contemporary materials. Designed to improve employee well-being and performance, offices and meeting rooms are located adjacent to open-plan, communal areas that encourage conversation and collaboration. Glass walls throughout underscore ideas of transparency and 100% of workspaces have access to daylight.

DIVERSITY
HUNGER
WAR OF

As exemplified by three distinct projects in La Jolla, Fort Worth, and Toledo, outcome-driven design is a focal point for HKS, not just the data it can leverage and the real-world insights its methodologies can produce, but for the experiences it can create for people–whether they're scientists, doctors, students, faculty, or administrative staff.

By cultivating a culture of continuous improvement, HKS refines its design processes across various projects. HKS employs diverse methods to gather feedback, including post-occupancy evaluations that assess how spaces perform in practice and sunlight studies that harness the light in sustainable ways to name just a few. The goal is not to acknowledge a job well done, but rather to understand what improvements can be made so they can influence future projects and enhance their ability to solve increasingly complex problems. Simply put, the qualitative and quantitative data and evaluations don't sit on a shelf. HKS uses them to shape future designs that support positive outcomes for patients, students, and employees by improving operational efficiency and promoting better mental and physical health.

Additionally, HKS actively engages with clients and stakeholders to adapt to their evolving needs, fostering innovative solutions that respond to changing environments. Every project is a testament to designers' dedication to sustainability, beauty, and how the built environment is perhaps the world's best testament to the concept of continuous improvement.

END NOTES

2. Congress Internationaux d'Architecture moderne (CIAM), *La Charte d'Athenes or The Athens Charter*, 1933. Trans J.Tyrwhitt. Paris, France: The Library of the Graduate School of Design, Harvard University, 1946.
3. Finance Fund, ProMedica Headquarters, accessed September 3, 2024, https://www.financefund.org/project/promedica-headquarters

SAN FRANCISCO INTERNATIONAL AIRPORT HARVEY MILK TERMINAL 1, BOARDING AREA B

B10
B11
B10 B11
B1 – B9
Exit
Baggage Claim
Restrooms
illy
BOURBON

SAN FRANCISCO INTERNATIONAL AIRPORT HARVEY MILK TERMINAL 1, BOARDING AREA B

CHOCOLATE COLLECTION

B9
11:14am
Southwest
1082
Las Vegas
oneworld

B

SAN FRANCISCO INTERNATIONAL AIRPORT HARVEY MILK TERMINAL 1, BOARDING AREA B

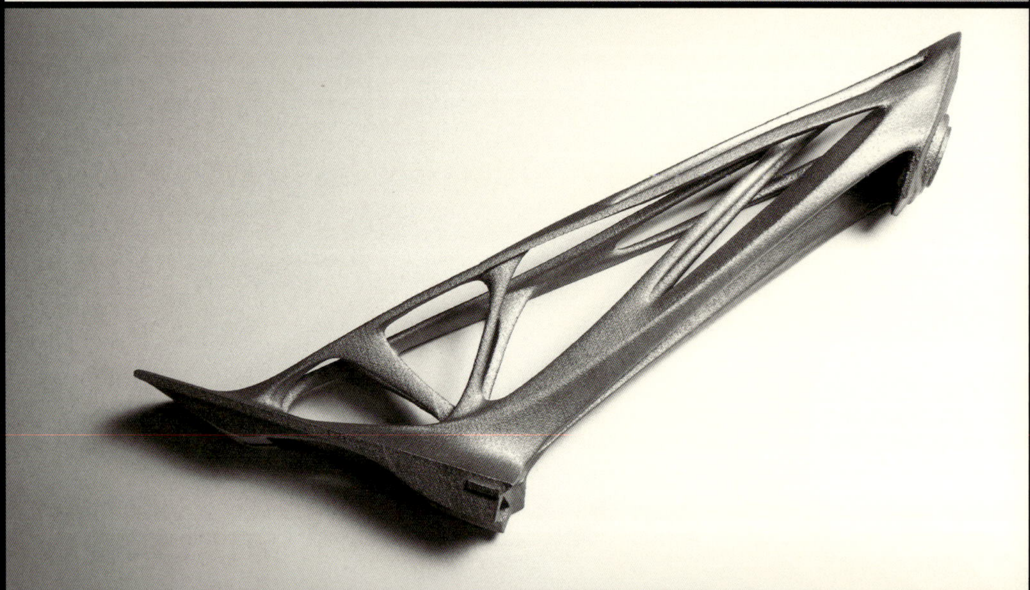

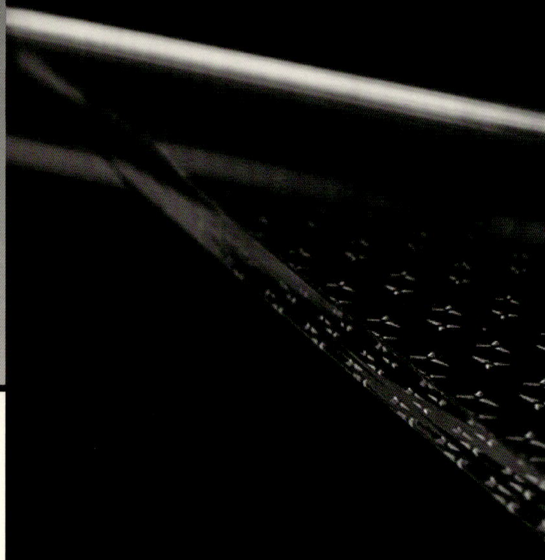

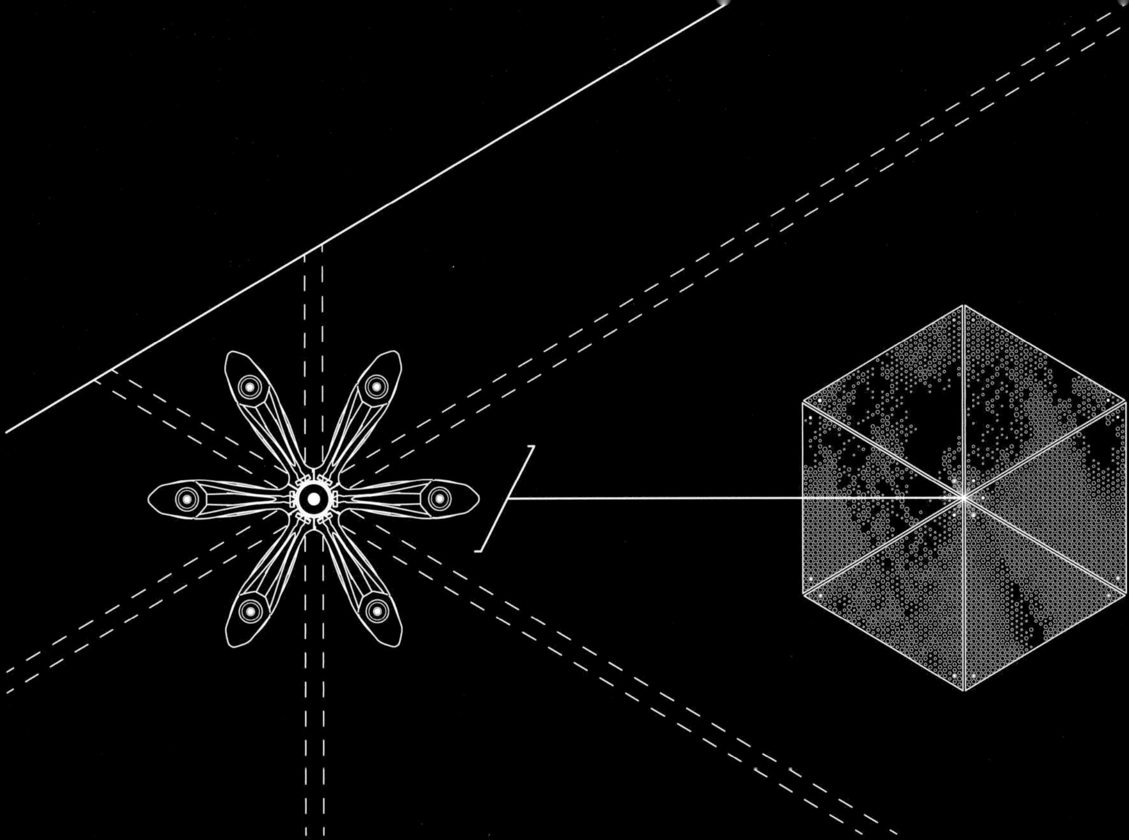

DIGITAL PROTOTYPING: When developing the design and digital delivery methodology for SoFi Stadium's roof, HKS used computational design tools to explore ways they could optimize the aluminum panel connections. The process helped them determine structural load capacity and drove aesthetics of the panel themselves.

REAL WORLD TESTING: By creating 3-D printed prototypes of metal connection nodes for SoFi Stadium roof panels, the HKS team was able to make discoveries that led to smarter, more efficient design and delivery decisions in the direct-to-fabrication collaboration with partners at Zahner.

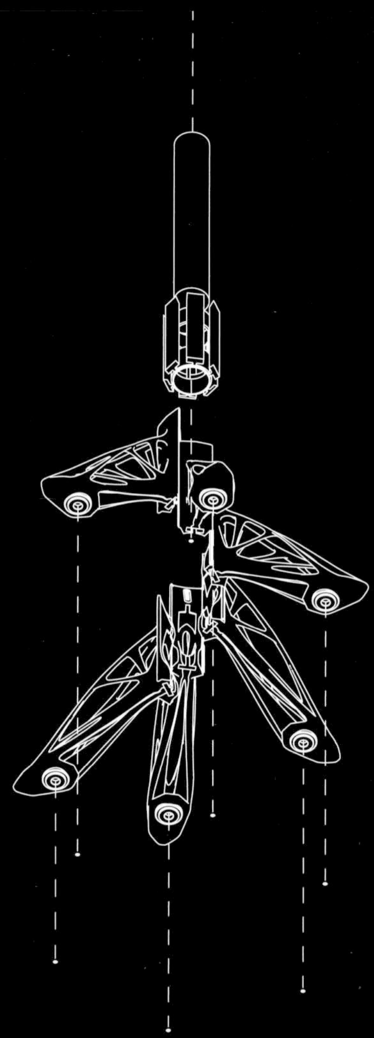

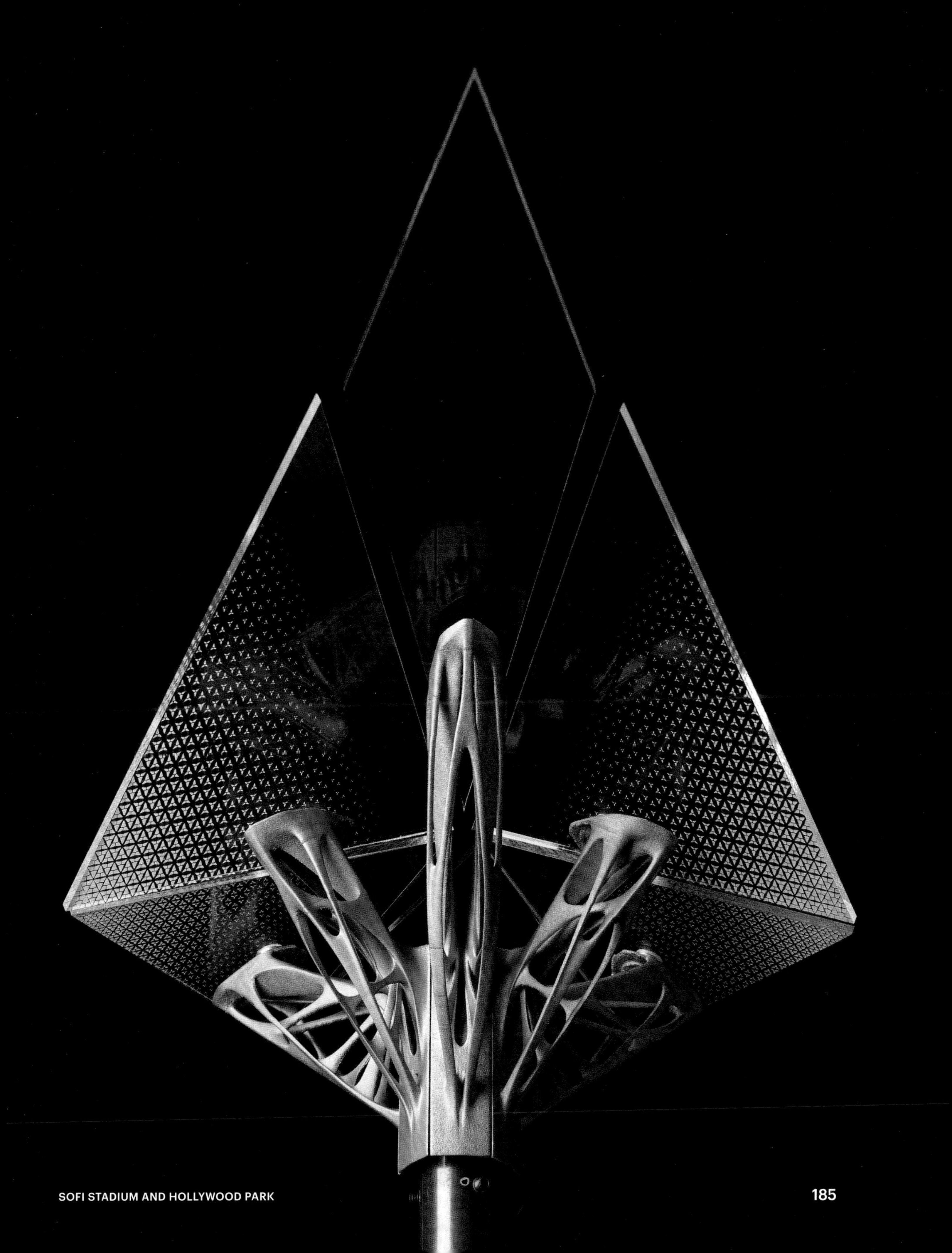

HIGH-PERFORMING SOLUTIONS: For the conceptual design of Rabat Ibn Sina Hospital, HKS teams conducted daylight and façade studies to develop designs solutions that reduce glare and heat gain and visually compelling making the hospital a comfortable, inviting place for everyone. The façade is designed to be white, a color that symbolizes health and cleanliness in Morocco.

Hospital Tower Façade

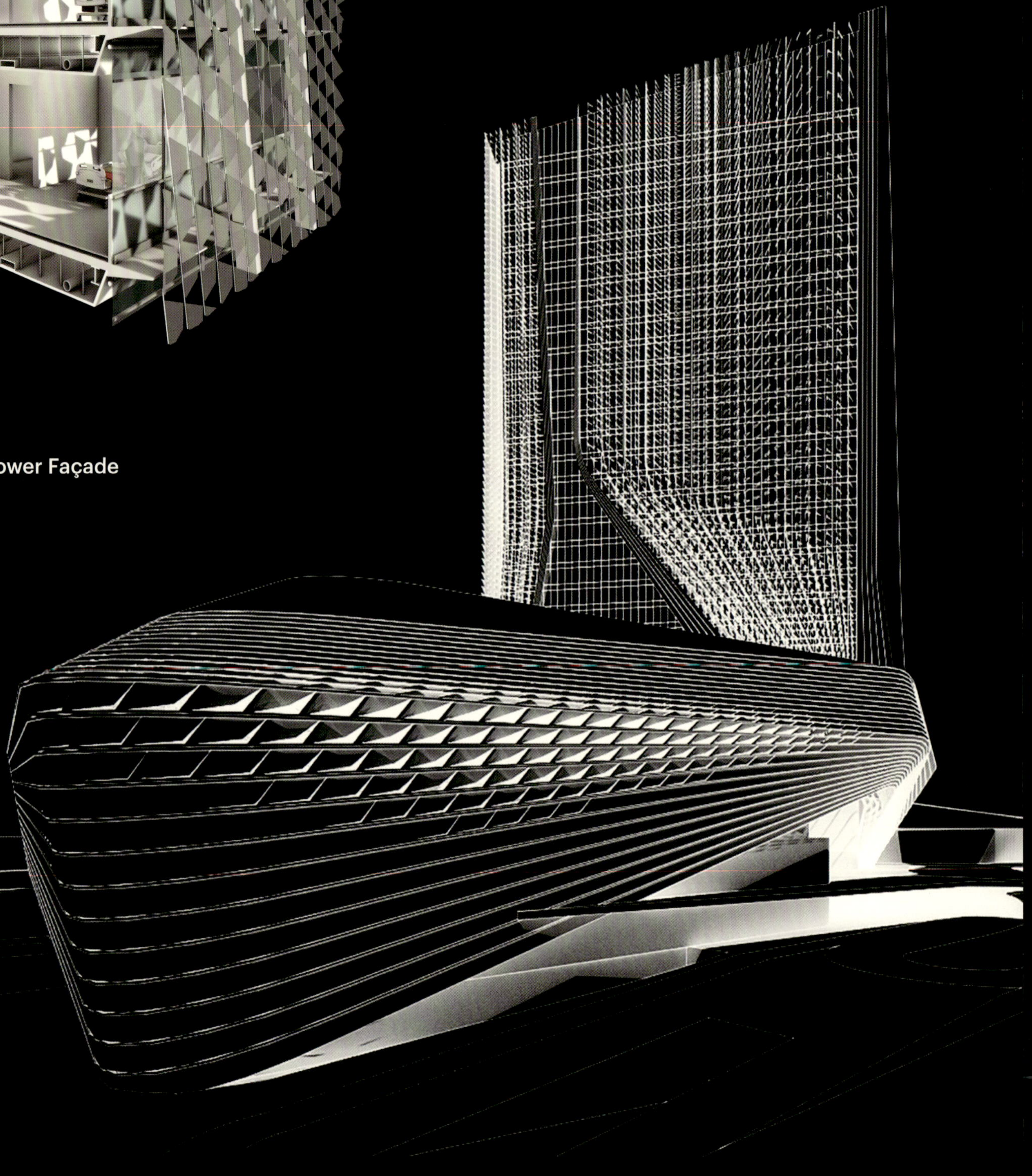

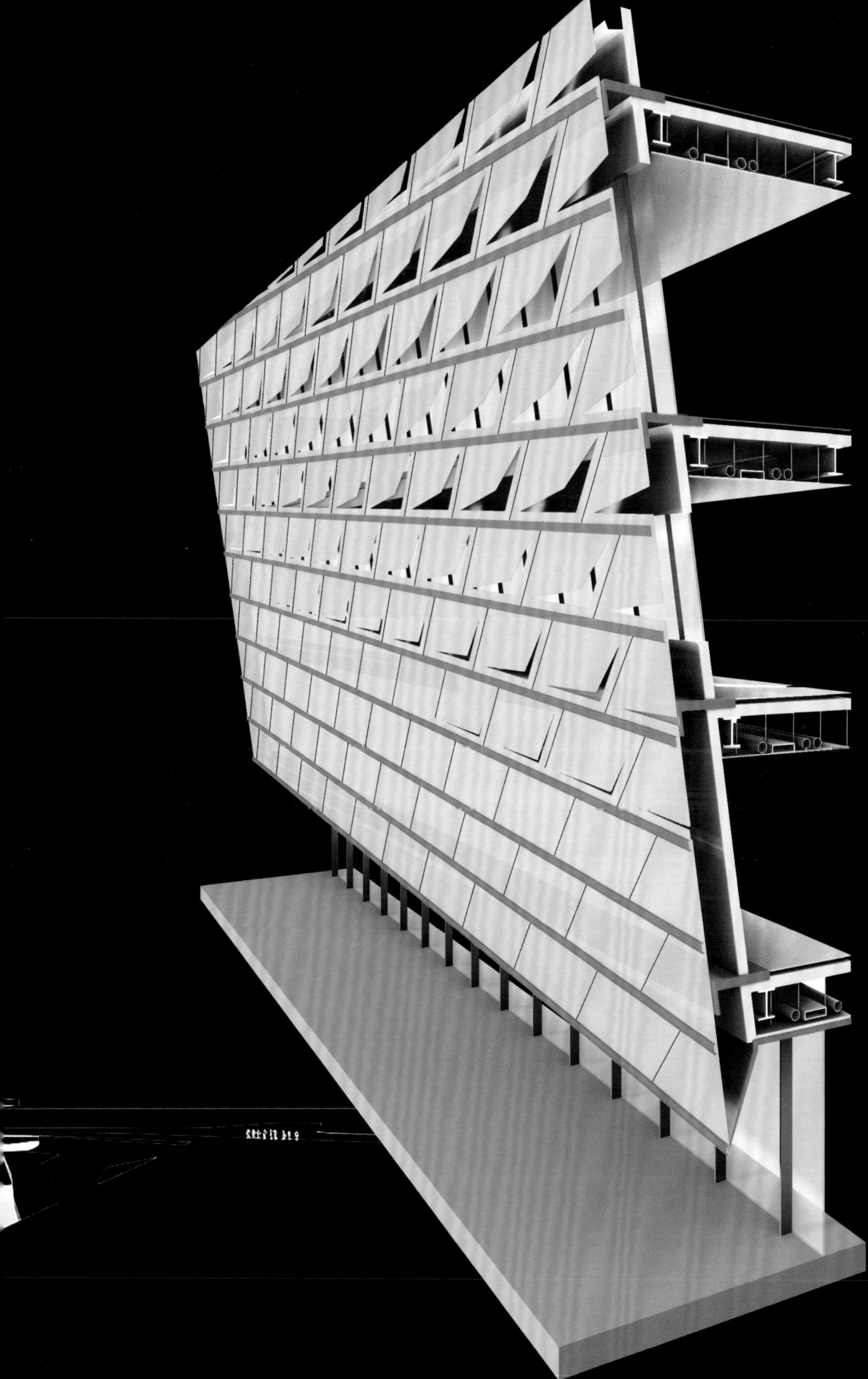

Podium Façade

TRANSFORMING HEALTH CARE: A new Dallas pediatric campus for Children's Health and UT Southwestern—designed through a partnership between HKS and Perkins & Will—will be one of the largest, most transformative pediatric hospitals in the nation. HKS' design for the master plan and bed towers are intended to make the health care environment feel calming, accessible and connected and promote restoration for children, families, and staff through integration with nature.

Pogue
Park

ROOMS WITH A VIEW: A view corridor study for the Children's Health and UT Southwestern Pediatric Campus included analyzing what portions of the building could be seen from far away, and how far people inside the building would be able to see out across Dallas. The study informed where public areas in the building are located to aid visual connectivity, and architectural features people would be able to see from the surrounding neighborhood.

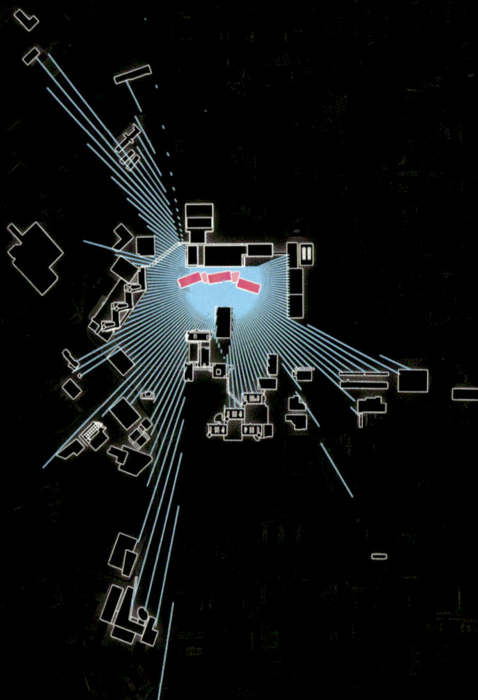

Views from Ground Level

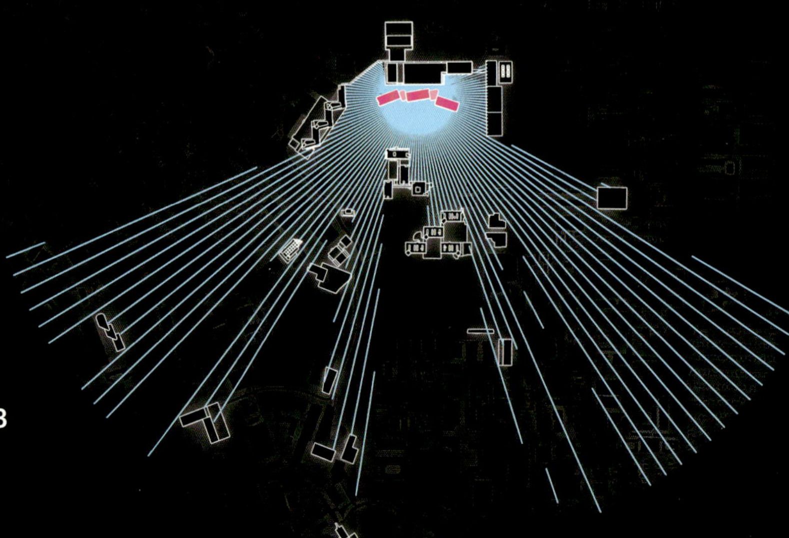

Views from Level 3

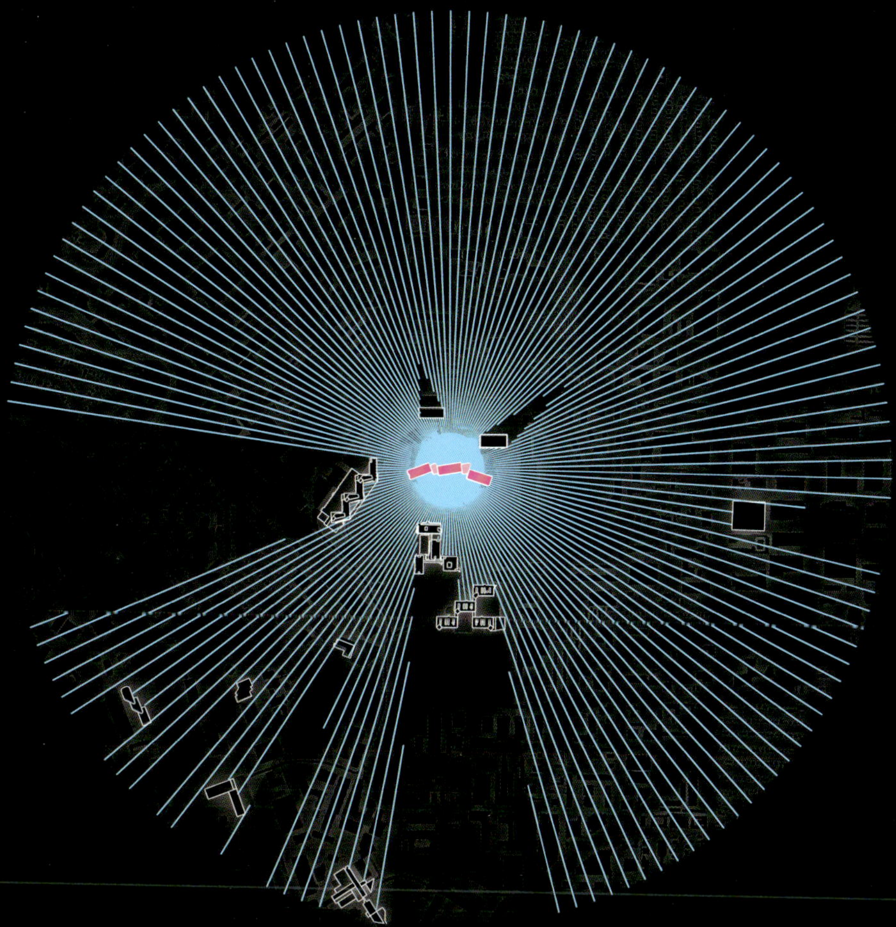

Views from Level 7

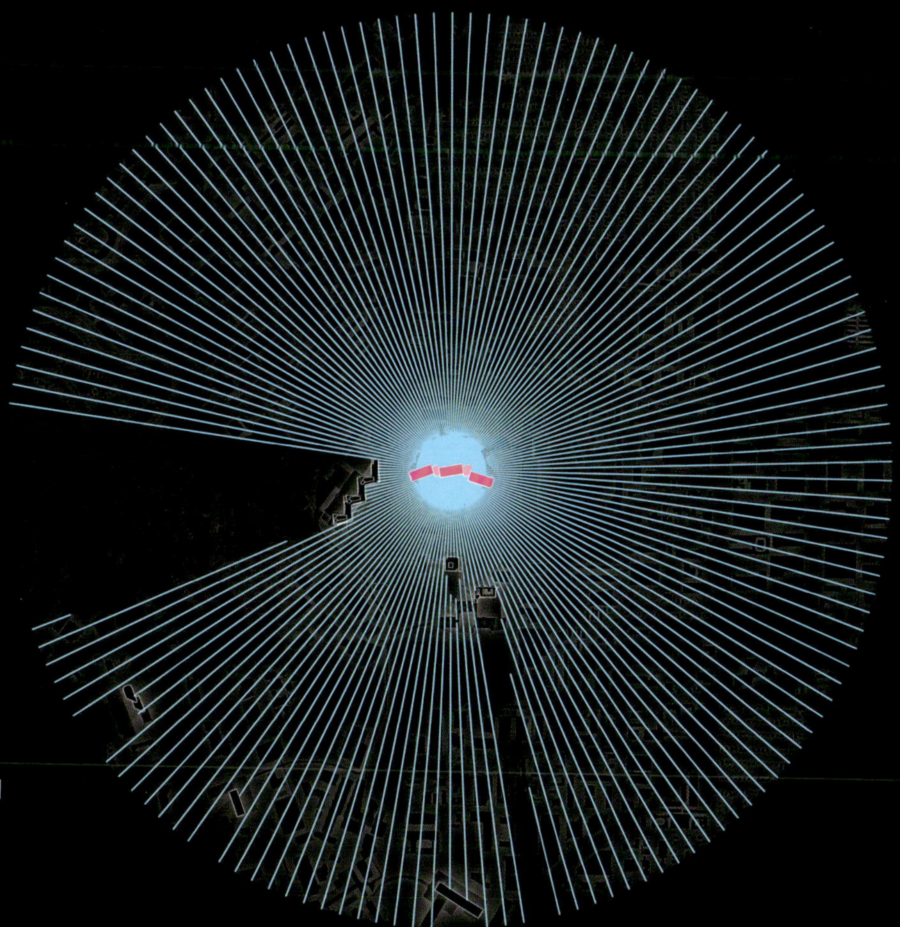

Views from Level 11

SUSTAINABLE BEAUTY: Texas Health Hospital Frisco and UT Southwestern Medical Center Frisco features a highly customized façade of precast concrete panels developed in part through computation design process that maximized resources and enabled smooth fabrication. The building also marks the first commercial application of mass timber in the city. Mass timber glulam V columns located at entry points and in the central breezeway create a warm and inviting atmosphere and are an environmentally responsible alternative to steel or concrete.

way Hospital
百汇医院

Parkway Hospital
百汇医院

1000
E. BROAD ST.

CHILDREN'S HOSPITAL OF RICHMOND AT VCU

GOVERNMENT CENTER
pulse

CHILDREN'S HOSPITAL OF RICHMOND AT VCU

3181C
B

ASU

COMMUNITY-SUPPORTED SCIENTIFIC RESEARCH: Developed through a partnership with Wexford Science & Technology, Arizona State University and the City of Phoenix, 850 Pheonix Bioscience Core is designed for world-class research and education, talent recruitment and retention, and community health and enrichment. The first and second floors include welcoming lobbies that can flex for large events, space for participant studies, clinical labs, a conference center, and research kitchen and a research fitness area.

DRIVING INNOVATION THROUGH INQUIRY

Image Credits

North Torrey Pines Living and Learning Neighborhood
Design: HKS, Inc. and Safdie Rabines Architects
Photography: © Tom Harris (132–135, 137 bottom, 138–139, 140 top, 141, 142–145); © Darren Bradley Photography (137 top, 140 bottom, 147)

Alcon Novartis Café
Photography: © Dror Baldinger, FAIA (148–150, 152–155, 158–159)

ProMedica Headquarters
Photography: © Tom Harris (160–169, 171, 172–175)

San Francisco International Airport Harvey Milk Terminal 1, Boarding Area B
Design: HKS, Inc. and Woods Bagot
Photography: © Jason O'Rear Photography (177, 180 top, 181); © Joe Fletcher (178–179, 180 bottom)

SoFi Stadium and Hollywood Park
Renderings and Prototypes: © HKS, Inc. (182–185)

St. Luke's Academic Medical Center
Renderings: © HKS, Inc. (186–187)

Rabat Ibn Sina Hospital
Renderings: © HKS, Inc. (188–193)

Children's Health and UT Southwestern Pediatric Campus
Design: HKS, Inc. and Perkins&Will
Renderings: © HKS, Inc. and Perkins&Will (194–199)
Studies: © HKS, Inc. (200–201)

Texas Health Hospital Frisco and UT Southwestern Medical Center Frisco
Photography: © HKS, Inc., Daryl Shields (202–203, 205); © Tom Harris (204)

ParkwayHealth Gleneagles Shanghai International Hospital
Photography: © Blackstation (206–211)

Children's Hospital of Richmond at VCU
Photography: © Garrett Rowland Photography (212–215)

Financial Institution Regional Headquarters
Photography: © Garrett Rowland Photography (216–223)

850 Phoenix Bioscience Core
Photography: © Nick Merrick Photographer (224–227, 232); © Bill Timmerman (228–231)

RETHINKING WHAT'S POSSIBLE

True innovation doesn't simply come from groundbreaking technologies. It requires a mindset of fearless curiosity, one that harnesses the powers of design thinking, technology, and old-fashioned problem solving.

HKS designers solve problems "within, through, beyond the built environment," which means they take a holistic view of how design relates to society's challenges, to the well-being of everyday people, and to the long-term impact buildings and spaces have on our shared world. It's an empathetic approach to innovation that celebrates collaboration and requires a commitment to client and community needs.

Even if its industry has historically lagged in research and development, HKS has invested time and energy into pursuing tools and ideas that can improve design processes and outcomes.

Artificial intelligence (AI) has grown by leaps and bounds in just the last few years for countless uses, including architectural design. AI, and the automation behind it, offers designers a model that learns, which can help them create environments that improve outcomes. Yes, recent advancements in these and other digital tools like Building Information Modeling (better-known by its acronym BIM) and digital twins are transforming design and construction. But at HKS, technological advancements are always guided by questions about improving the lives of the people who encounter buildings and spaces created by the firm's multidisciplinary designers.

Thinking holistically is also about forcing yourself to change your perspective, which is why HKS designers often position themselves as strategic advisors rather than service-oriented problem solvers. Why is this important? The industry faces growing complexity due to challenges like labor shortages, environmental concerns, and changing client expectations. To tackle these issues, all of the disciplines that relate to design must be integrated to maximize the positive impacts design has on people and their spaces. This requires a view of design that considers not only aesthetic or functional aspects but also long-term goals for occupant health, sustainability, and resilience, which can improve the overall lifecycle of a building.

Thinking beyond the building, HKS teams use their training and talent to offer new ideas for what the built environment can be—structures that don't always fit the common perception of what architects contribute and modular solutions that can be repeated to achieve the high standard of performance. Immersive technology, virtual reality and the metaverse, or 3D digital worlds where people interact via avatars, help HKS designers find those optimal solutions in real time and offer a new frontier for design that transcends the physical realm.

At HKS, innovation requires more than generating ideas—it demands a commitment to change, embracing agility, collaboration, and experimentation. It's about a fundamental passion for problem-solving and a commitment to curiosity to push the bounds of what design can do.

PACIFIC PLAZA

MAKING LIFE MORE COMFORTABLE: Pacific Plaza Pavilion and its surrounding park are part of a broader movement in Dallas to transform sites into green space and ease the effects of soaring temperatures in the city, which average ninety-six degrees Fahrenheit in the shade in peak summer. The pavilion structure tempers the microclimate around it: the buffed steel reduces glare for the offices above and the morse code-inspired punctures diffuse the sunlight to create shade below, making it slightly cooler than the surrounding downtown area.

Fearless curiosity has come to define the firm in recent years as it approaches the centennial anniversary of its 1939 founding. Just as the firm has expanded to offices around the world in that time, its work has expanded beyond the confines of traditional architectural practice.

This progress is perhaps best exemplified by Pacific Plaza Pavilion, located in a park adjacent to HKS' downtown Dallas headquarters, an area that had undergone a rapid transformation in recent years. HKS was challenged to create a useful and contextual structure for the new park, befitting this Lazarus story of a site that used to be a surface parking lot. Useful, that is, for more than 135,000 workers who report to nearby offices each day, and contextual for this former terminus of the Texas and Pacific Railways.

Fueled by an interest in the site's history and the pursuit of using nascent technology to model a climate-responsive and unique structural design, the HKS design team created a signature circular form to serve as a pavilion. Defined by a ring of bead-blasted stainless steel held aloft by steel pillars and punctured in a pattern that mimics a map of old local railway stops in American Morse Code, the design pays homage to the days when telegraphers stationed in railway depots would send messages to train crews and dispatchers.

Since its opening in 2019, the pavilion has offered a place for people to rest, served as a focal point for a new downtown park, and honored the site's past as an economic boon for one of Texas' most vibrant cities.

"We just hoped it would be embraced, but in the end, people are creating memories for themselves there," says Jon Bailey, a Practice Design Director for HKS' Laboratory for INtensive Exploration (LINE).

Creating places for memories is a beautiful outcome of how HKS designers work across the firm's many practices and services with the belief that better cities and communities are possible through design innovation. By building strategic relationships with local organizations and governments in cities worldwide, designers are strengthening how the built environment can support people.

PlainsCapital Bank

Like with Pacific Plaza Pavilion in Dallas, HKS designers have sought to transform public space in Atlanta, on a pro bono project dubbed StationSoccer. A partnership among local non-profit Soccer in the Streets, the Metropolitan Atlanta Rapid Transit Authority (MARTA), the Department of City Planning and the Atlanta United Foundation, and HKS developed a cohesive vision for Station Soccer: a multi-site masterplan that transforms underutilized land near several transit stations into youth soccer fields and community program sites.

Through research and engagement workshops, the HKS team developed a unique program and design for each station that honors the identity and culture of the surrounding community. Stations—which HKS also raised funds for—may feature a garden, a learning center inside a decommissioned MARTA rail car, a mobile health truck or event space, all of which are included in a "kit of parts" that allows customization for each neighborhood's needs and aspirations.

"Sometimes a gratifying experience in the real estate profession does not involve a building, but it always involves people," says Sheba Ross, Global Practice Director of Cities and Communities and a partner at HKS, speaking of the StationSoccer initiative.

StationSoccer represents a strategy that enables designers to maximize resources and provide unique, contextual spaces through replicable, scalable and sustainable solutions. HKS takes this approach to support diverse industries, creating modular solutions for data centers and technology companies, commercial clients and health care systems to name just a few.

Since nearly 140 million ER visits are logged each year in the United States, HKS wanted to create a way for doctors and nurses to deliver acute treatment effectively and efficiently, while balancing patient privacy and comfort. What one design and research team conceived of was just that: a reproducible product called the COVE™ Treatment Area, now a collaboration with production partner DIRTT.

The semi-private spaces for examinations, treatments, and healing are one-third the size of the average exam room resemble pods. With a purple glow, reclining chair, and flexible medical device accommodations, they take everything we know about therapeutic solutions to support each patient's journey, while being cost-effective and increasing capacity for health organizations.

For Chicago's Northwestern Memorial Hospital, the HKS team designed the first set of the pods that ultimately inspired Cove™ to be more than a welcomed solution for healthcare providers. It designed pods to help patients rebalance their expectations for personalized care and comfort in a setting that is often one of the most difficult places a person can wind up.

A	East Lake Marta Station
B	Pedestrian Crossing
C	Artwalk
D	Community Garden
E	Mobile Health Truck
F	Library Pavilion and Shade Structure
G	Event Plaza

TRANSIT-ORIENTED TRANSFORMATION: Each StationSoccer site in Atlanta is designed to have amenities local community members want and need ranging from mobile health units to pavilions. One design aspect is constant, though—every location has brand-new soccer fields that help close the play equity gap in the city. The East Lake location (above) features diverse community spaces and the Kensington location (right), once a parking lot, is now filled with vibrant murals.

CREATE
A
B
C
D
E
F
G

UNSTOPPABLE

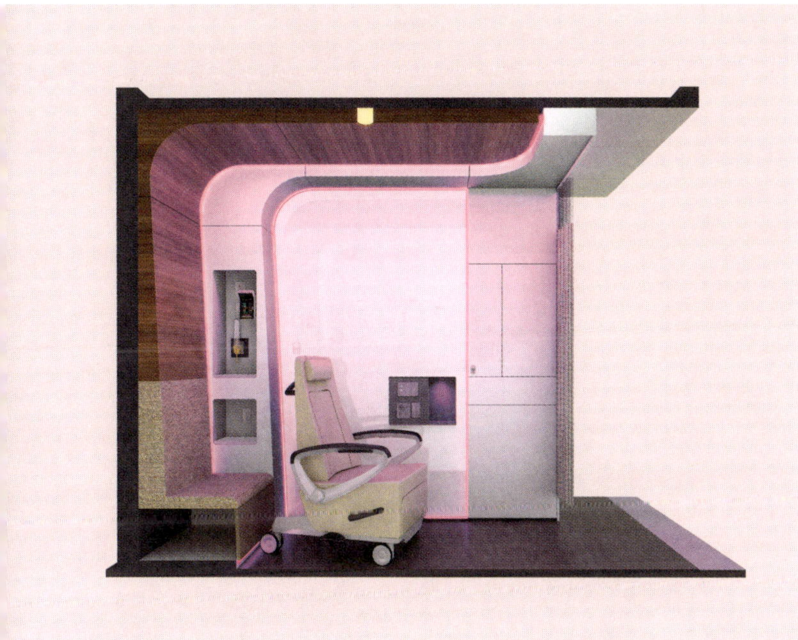

ITERATING AND IMPROVING: Throughout the design and development process for COVE™ Treatment Areas, HKS conducted several prototype and mockup evaluations, yielding feedback from patients and providers. The team learned how the modular approach worked, where components could be optimally located, and how to make improvements to durability without driving up cost or sacrificing comfort. They also corrected some of their assumptions about how acoustics would work—at first thinking curves in the design would deflect ambient noise, but then realizing sound needed to be absorbed instead.

COVE™ succeeds in optimizing care and creating a restorative experience, while delivering a design-forward solution to the most fundamental musts such as infection prevention in its use and carbon reduction in its manufacture. As HKS' first patent-to-product design project out in the market, it demonstrates the value that design thinking can bring to transforming the built environment as well as operations and care.

"It's new ground because of our collaboration with DIRTT—we have our sights set on this being an industry solution for patients and ER departments," says Deborah Wingler, Global Practice Director of Applied Research and a principal at HKS. "HKS has started to think about productization in other ways after this project."

HKS had deployed similar research and design strategies as those applied for COVE™ in 2017, when it designed the first sensory well-being hub at Lane Tech College Prep High School in Chicago to help neurodiverse students recover from environmental stressors and refocus on classroom learning. In addition to designing the hub pro bono, HKS helped raise funds for its construction.

When the hub was built, HKS then studied how students engaged with the structure's interactive art and soundscape and its calming cocoon, finding that many young people—especially those who are neurodivergent or autistic—desired diverse spaces and ways to engage that would make them feel comfortable and safe. The team eventually created an open-source design guide so other schools, organizations and designers could build their own hubs, and in the time since, HKS has created similar environments for projects ranging from children's hospitals to airports.

"The beauty of the modular design is its flexibility; it can be replicated in different settings without the need for hard construction," says Lisa Adams, Director of Citizen HKS, a Sustainable Design Leader for Interiors and principal at HKS,

While the hubs are small in stature, suited to provide space for just a few who need their comforts, they are representative of a bigger movement that HKS is spearheading to provide engaging sensory experiences at all scales and touch people with the power of design. Whether they are students at school, patients in a clinical setting, or sports fans enjoying a game, the people who engage with spaces designed by HKS get to see, hear, feel, and experience life in new ways.

Following this path of discovery, HKS was selected by Cosm for the design of its new venues for immersive live events, in what can only be described as an industry-leading move. In some sense, Cosm venues—the first two of which opened in 2024 in Los Angeles and Dallas—are buildings designed for entertainment, but

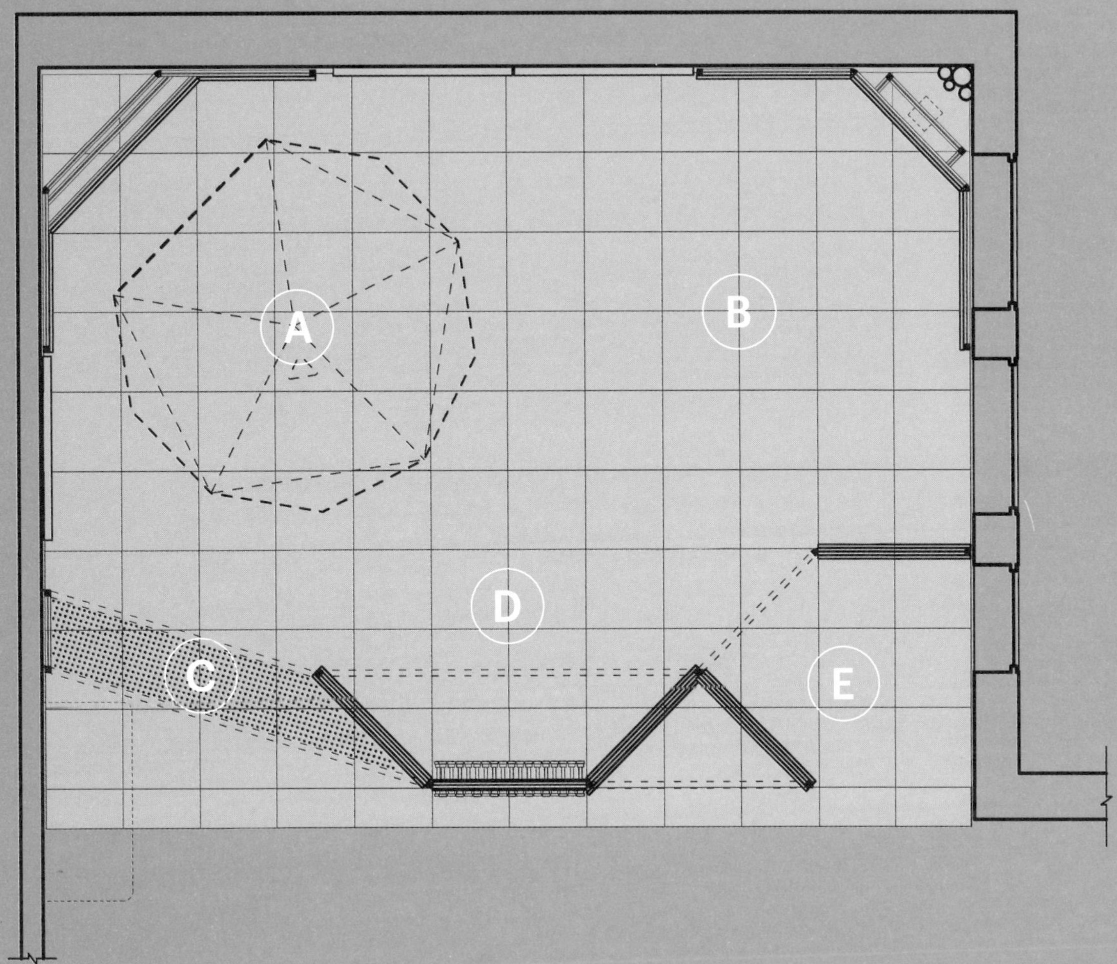

OPEN-SOURCE DESIGN: The sensory well-being hub consists of zones for both activity and respite that can feature soothing audio, lighting, and biophilic videos that enable students to escape the occasionally overwhelming school environment and find peace in solitude. The first cocoon structure was designed computationally with 3D printed nodes which allows for easy movement. An open-source design guide published by HKS details how similar structures can be replicated by schools and other organizations.

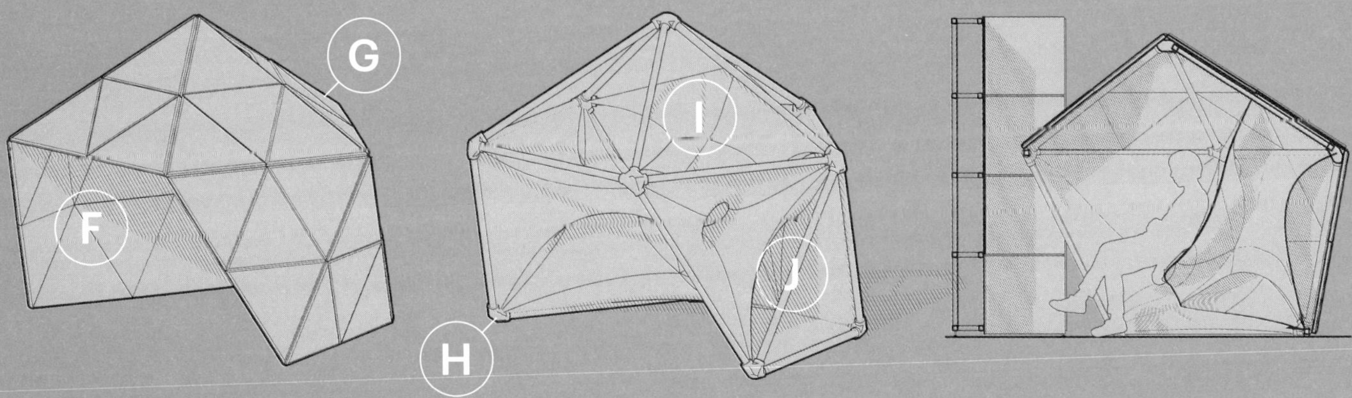

A	Cocoon Zone
B	Respite Zone
C	Tactile Zone
D	Active Zone
E	Open Access Point

F	Cocoon Enclosure
G	Acoustic Panels
H	Connector Nodes
I	Tensile Fabric
J	Aluminum Framing

A SOOTHING MICROENVIRONMENT: The sensory well-being hub's cocoon structure is a semi-enclosed microenvironment with seating double-layered acoustic panels and a tensile fabric designed and fabricated by Sean Ahlquist, Associate Professor of Architecture at University of Michigan's Taubman College of Architecture and Urban Planning. The design elements come together to provide a physically and mentally soothing atmosphere for students.

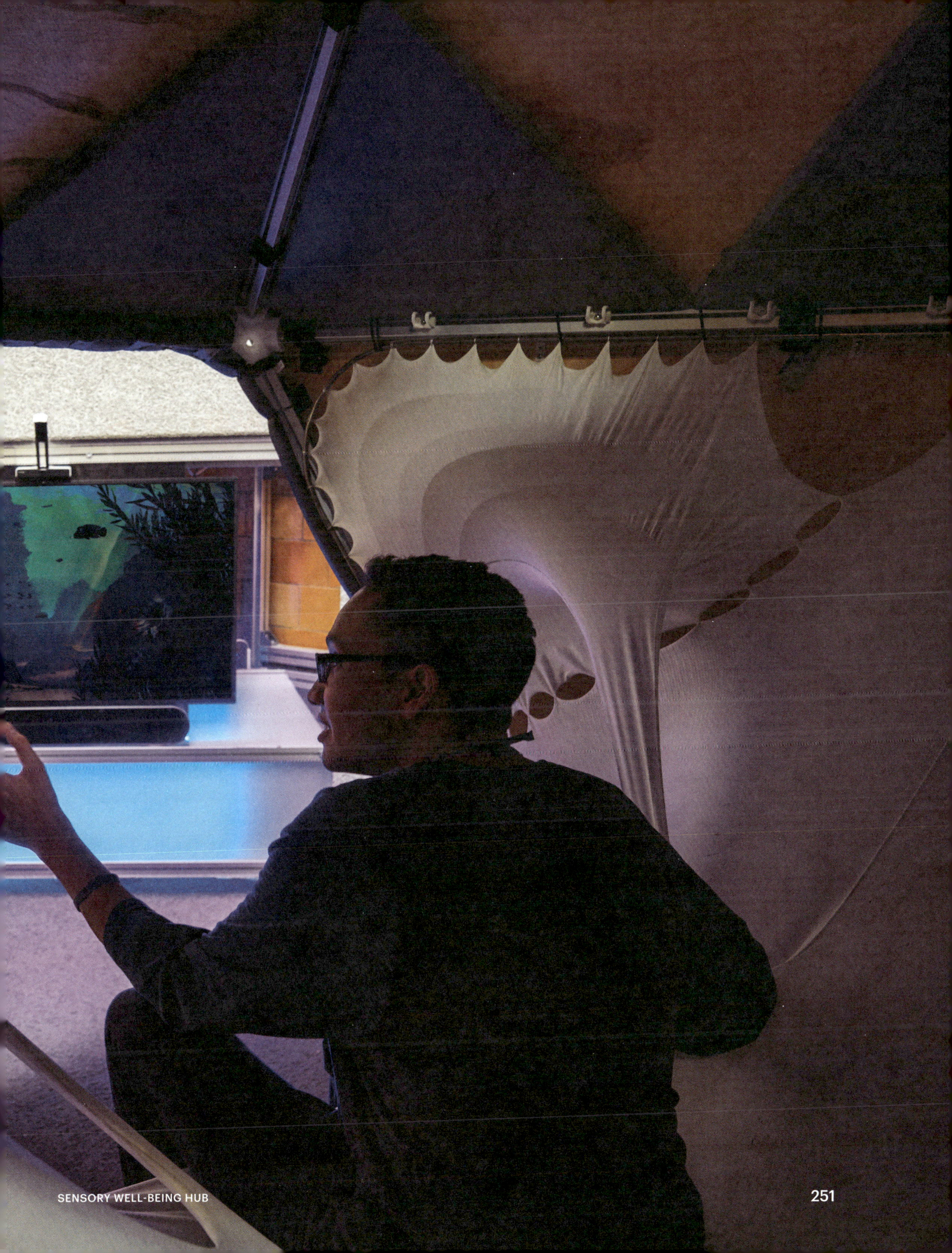

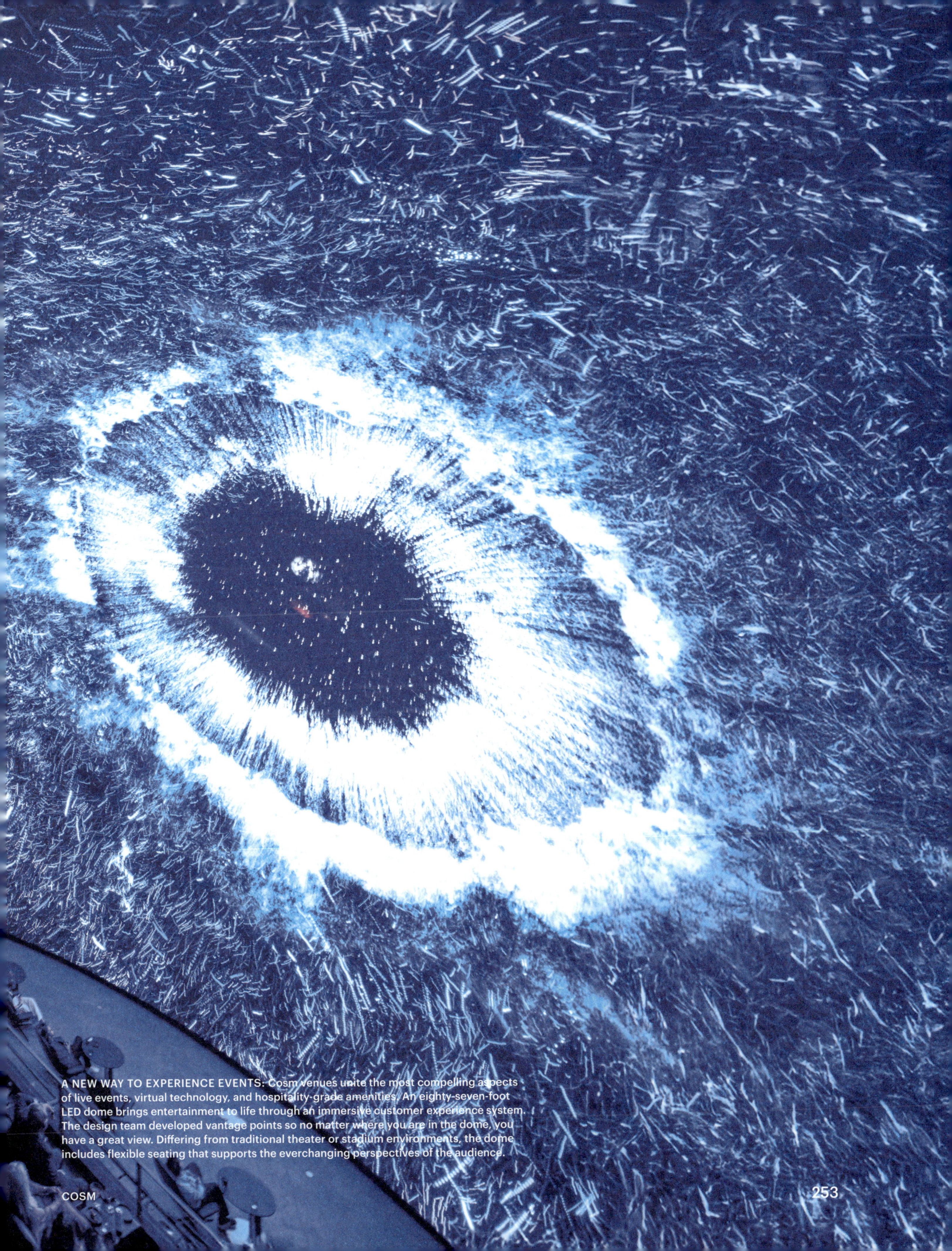

A NEW WAY TO EXPERIENCE EVENTS: Cosm venues unite the most compelling aspects of live events, virtual technology, and hospitality-grade amenities. An eighty-seven-foot LED dome brings entertainment to life through an immersive customer experience system. The design team developed vantage points so no matter where you are in the dome, you have a great view. Differing from traditional theater or stadium environments, the dome includes flexible seating that supports the everchanging perspectives of the audience.

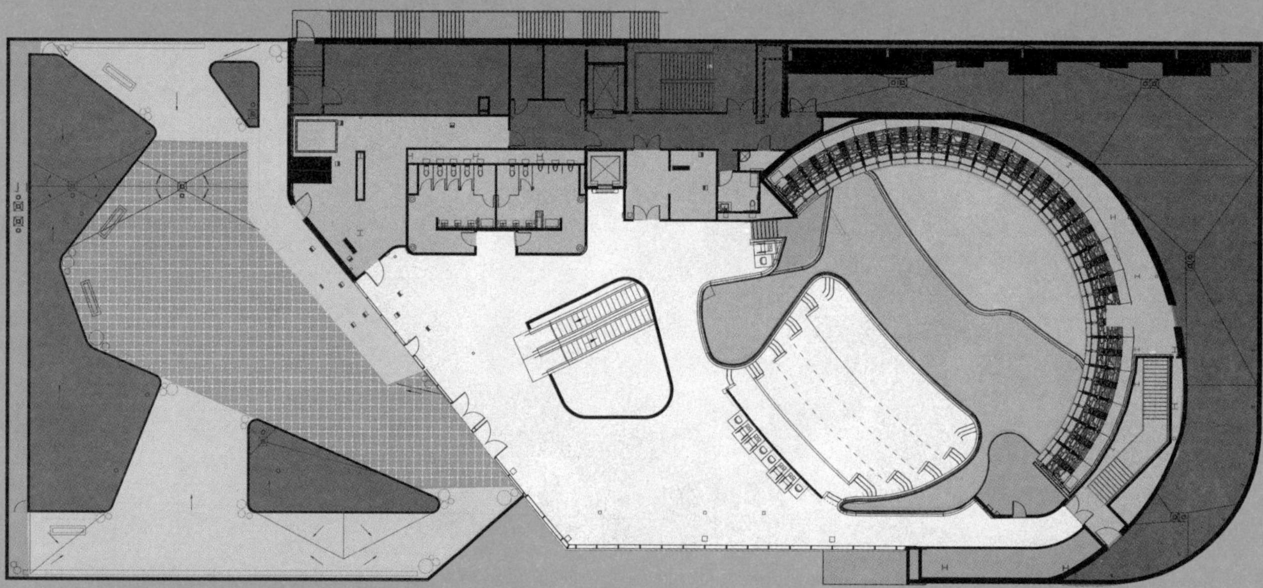

Level 3

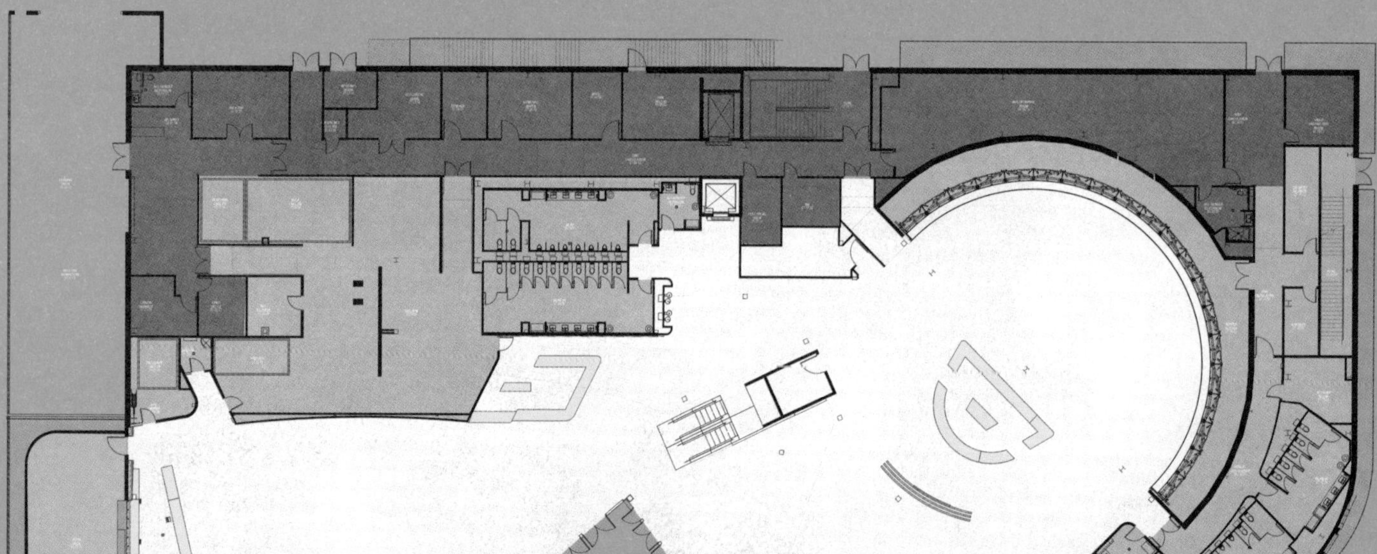

Level 1

Cosm Dallas

Cosm Los Angeles

VIRTUAL REALITY AS A DESIGN TOOL: HKS immersive technologists created a metaverse version of the Atlanta office to amplify the benefits of using visualization in the design process. The digital experience they created built awareness among the firm's global employees about the future of work and the workplace.

in another sense, they are a completely new type of venue designed to transport fans right to the middle of the action of a game or arts and entertainment event.

Centered around Cosm's Shared Reality technology, which brings immersive experiences to physical spaces, the venues feature diverse indoor and outdoor spaces where patrons can freely move about to customize—and maximize—the time they spend there.

Cosm's vision includes creating venues that lean into regional aesthetics and culture, so they are approachable and relevant for local audiences. Situated in Hollywood Park next to SoFi Stadium, Cosm L.A. features a distinctly Southern Californian white plaster exterior, art deco touches, and a deck that maximizes the indoor/outdoor lifestyle of Angelinos. Cosm Dallas, located in The Colony, has a façade crafted with local Texas limestone and is seamlessly woven into the existing Grandscape development.

Cosm's venues unite the most compelling aspects of live events, immersive technology, and hospitality-grade amenities for unparalleled, accessible fan experiences in Shared Reality.

"We are known for creating innovative environments for people to experience sports and entertainment. Through our partnership with Cosm, we've elevated the convergence of the physical and virtual world," says Mark A. Williams, Global Sector Director of Venues and a partner and executive vice president at HKS.

Elevating the convergence of the physical and digital world is not something HKS teams reserve just for their final products. In fact, with each passing day, technologists within the firm create new methods of activating digital modeling and visualization. By creating virtual environments, HKS teams test and validate design ideas and collaborate with clients and users, to build emotional connections that make a space feel real before it exists in the real world.

When companies around the globe, including HKS, re-evaluated office real estate portfolios in the aftermath of the COVID-19 pandemic given the way it transformed hybrid work, visualization became a central component of how the firm's designers pursued creative solutions for workplaces. Using insights from the firm's research about the future of work—which explored the notion that the office has evolved from a place into an ecosystem comprising people, policy, processes, technology, and the built environment—the HKS Atlanta team designed a new workplace for itself.

Along the way, immersive technology specialists created a metaverse version of the new office to share design concepts in a live platform for HKS' global employees to experience. The goals were multifold: to educate fellow designers about how they could bring more value to clients with visualization, amplify the benefits virtual environments could have for user experience, and to inspire others to reimagine work ecosystems in their own home cities.

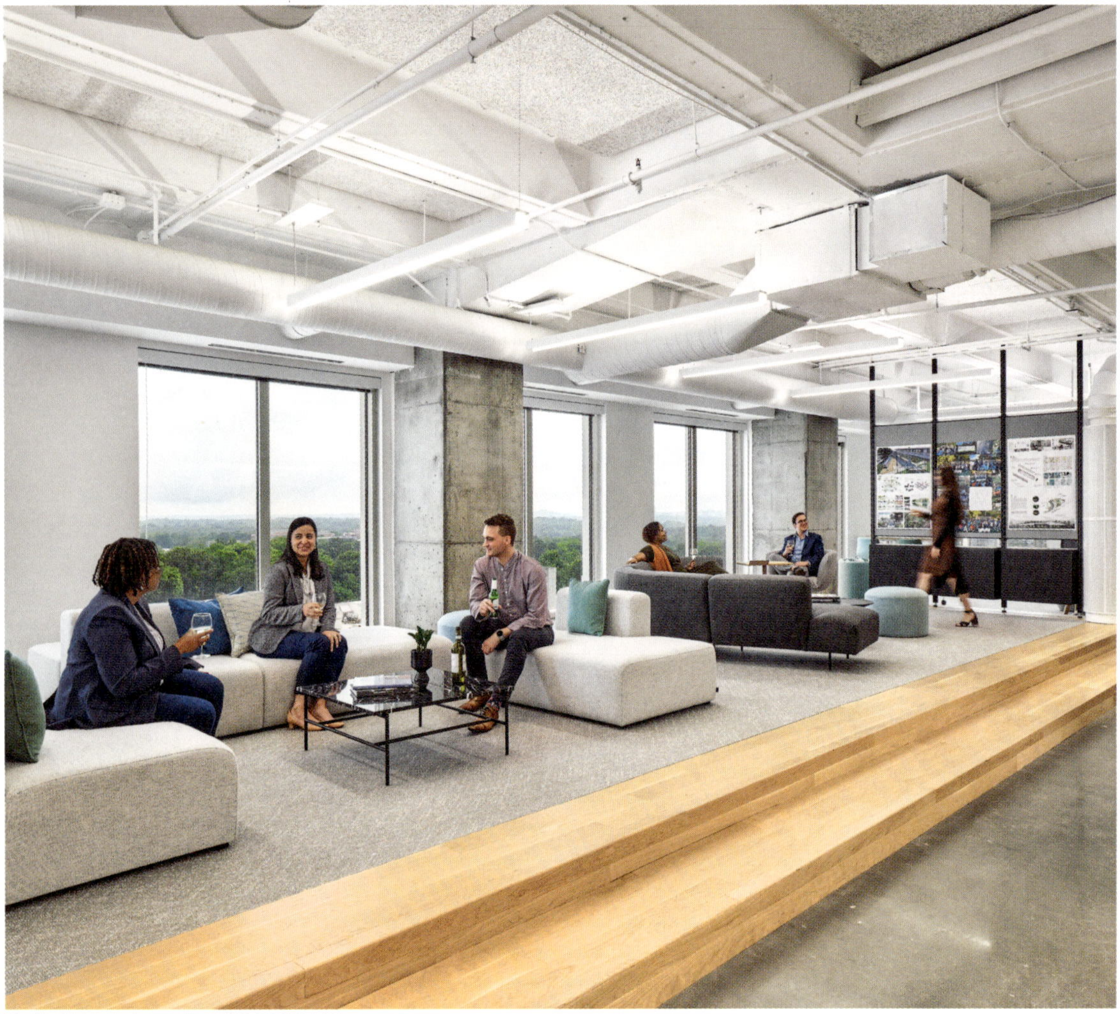

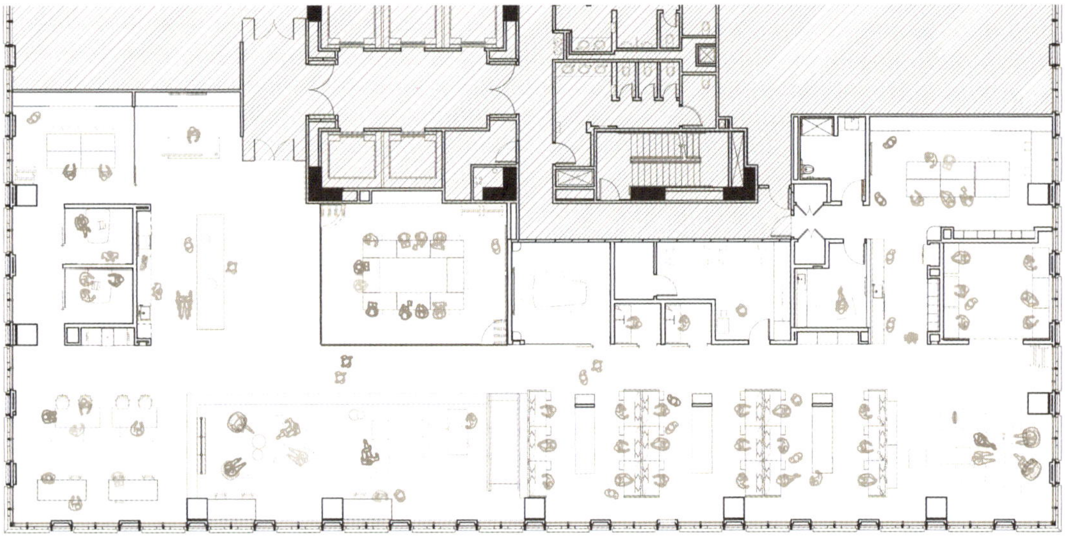

BRAIN HEALTHY DESIGN: Through a partnership with The Center for BrainHealth, HKS conducted a study to evaluate brain health in the workplace and created a framework of five affordances that workplaces can provide to support employee brain health: focus, exploration & ideation, collaboration & co-creation, rest & reflection, and social connection. HKS has applied design strategies that enable these affordances in commercial interiors projects such as the firm's Atlanta office. A follow up study on the office revealed that the new design and behavioral changes resulted in a 17.5 percent decrease in multitasking frequency and a 36.7 percent increase in the number of focused tasks completed each day among Atlanta team members.

"We were thinking about a holistic work environment where we come together to create, collaborate, meet with clients and produce and deliver our work," says Atlanta Office Director and a partner at HKS, Julie Volosin, of the workplace design.

Though it now exists in the real world–in a commercial office building in Atlanta's Buckhead neighborhood–the new workplace exemplifies how HKS approaches the idea of designing within, through and beyond the built environment. It features an idea theater for creative work sessions and events, rapid ops rooms for project teams on deadlines and havens where colleagues can work independently or take breaks–all spaces created to support holistic employee well-being inspired by findings from the firm's industry-leading brain healthy workplace research.

HKS is now leading the industry forward with its commitment to brain health, convening scientists, community organizations, companies and policymakers to ensure that as technology advances and influences how our environments are shaped, critical thinking, ethical considerations, and empathy remain an indispensable part of building our shared world.

If brains are the engines that fuel creativity and innovation, then HKS demonstrates leadership by safeguarding their invaluable, and powerful, role in design. As the firm continues its pursuit of innovation and creating positive change in communities around the world, the synergy between human creativity and technology holds a promise that designers are using to forge a meaningful path forward.

Architecture offers us, as a society, a way of building. And design, as both a process and a product, can transform society with its possibilities, extending far beyond the creation of mere spaces.

By considering the broader context of societal challenges and the long-term impact of buildings, HKS adopts a holistic view that prioritizes both people and the planet. HKS teams make connections that enrich individual experiences, spark inspiration, and strengthen the vital links that make communities thrive.

By conducting empirical research, leveraging data and real-world insights to guide them, HKS designers ensure that their decisions are rooted in outcomes. They evaluate those outcomes to inform the future, creating a prosperous, connected cycle of improvement.

And by conceiving of their work as extending "within, through, beyond the built environment" HKS expands the boundaries of traditional design practice. Leveraging new technology and forging a path toward progress, the firm's designers create custom tools and novel approaches in an industry that holds a great responsibility to impact lives.

Design is a powerful catalyst for positive change. This philosophy lies at the heart of HKS' practice. The firm's global teams foster collaboration, address client and community needs, and create spaces that promote well-being while contributing to a more sustainable, connected world. Together, they design places that not only meet today's needs but also contribute to a better tomorrow.

RETHINKING WHAT'S POSSIBLE

AUTOCAMP

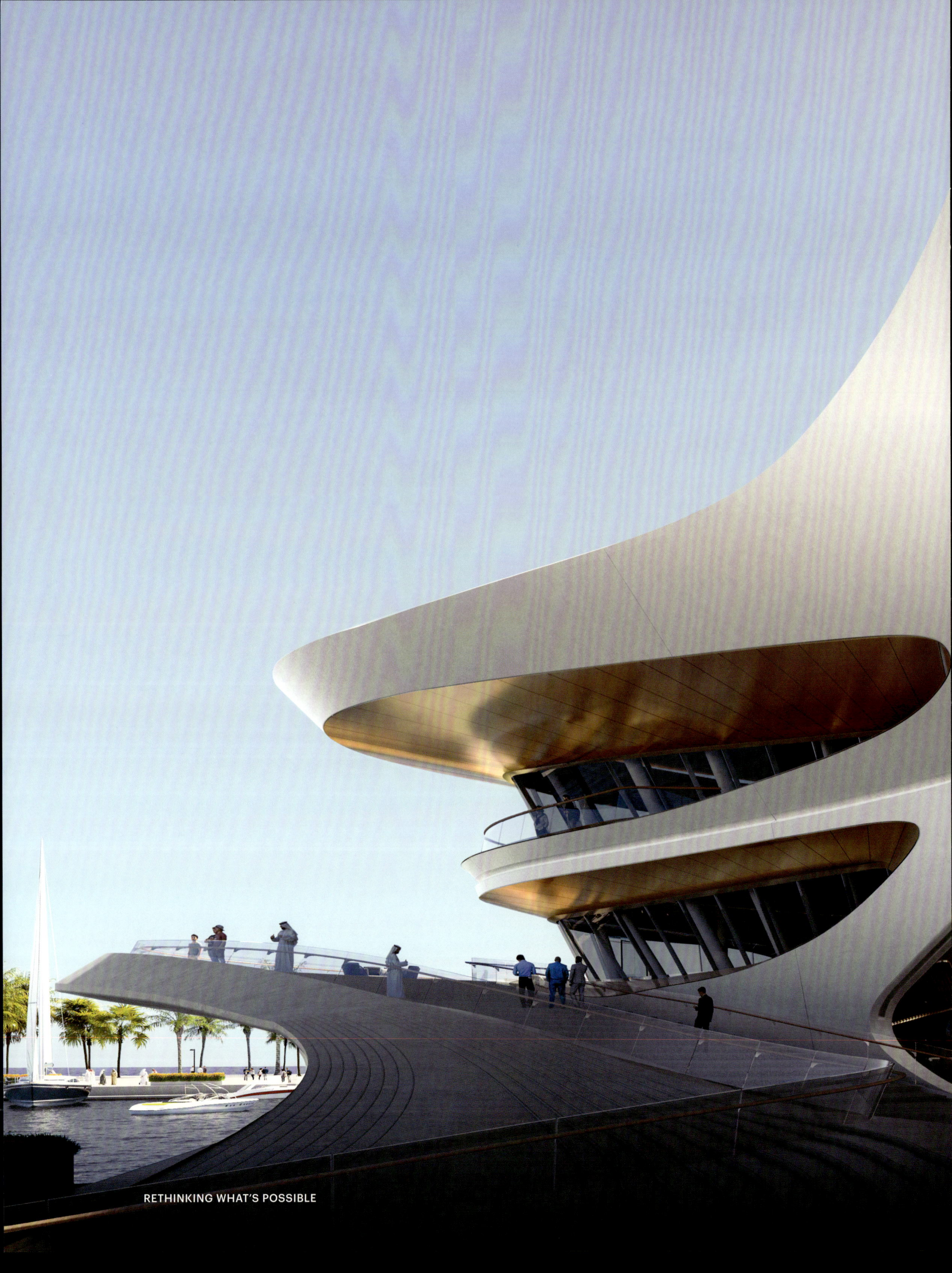

INSPIRED BY LAND AND SEA: AMAALA Triple Bay Marina Yacht Club in Saudi Arabia forms a gateway to the Red Sea and provides public access to the waterfront. The design's curved forms and cantilevered terraces are influenced by maritime history and unique rock formations on the nearby coastline and cliffs. The luxury members club welcomes local and global travelers through an arch that creates a shaded plaza and frames dramatic water views.

BLACKS

RETHINKING WHAT'S POSSIBLE

A CULTURAL DESTINATION: The Arena in Diriyah in Riyadh is designed for residents of the Kingdom of Saudi Arabia and visitors who want to connect with Nadji culture. The architecture is a composition of stone monoliths that rise from the landscape and evoke local geological formations and ancient Najdi forts and palaces. Digital waterfall features animated by light serve as a beacon drawing guests to the dynamic experience inside.

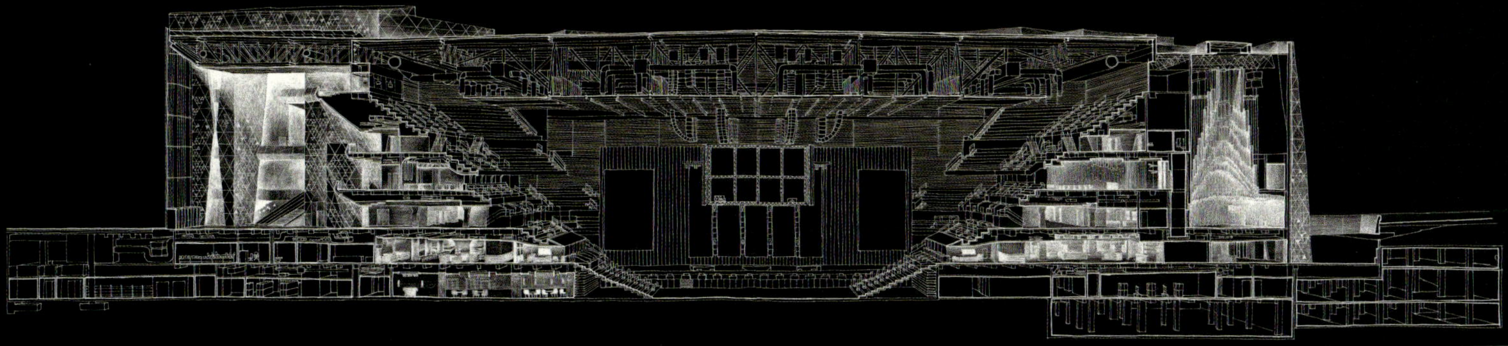

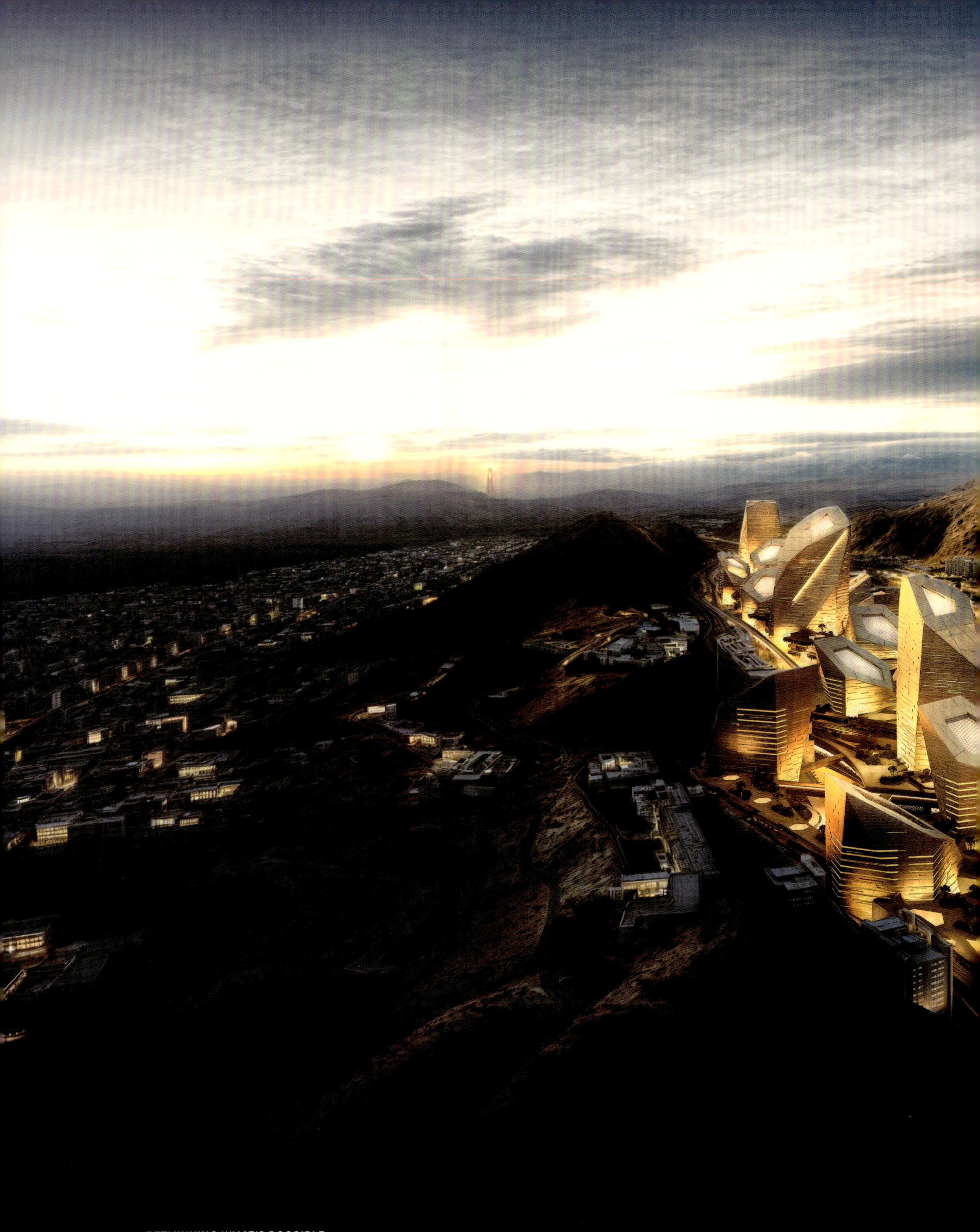

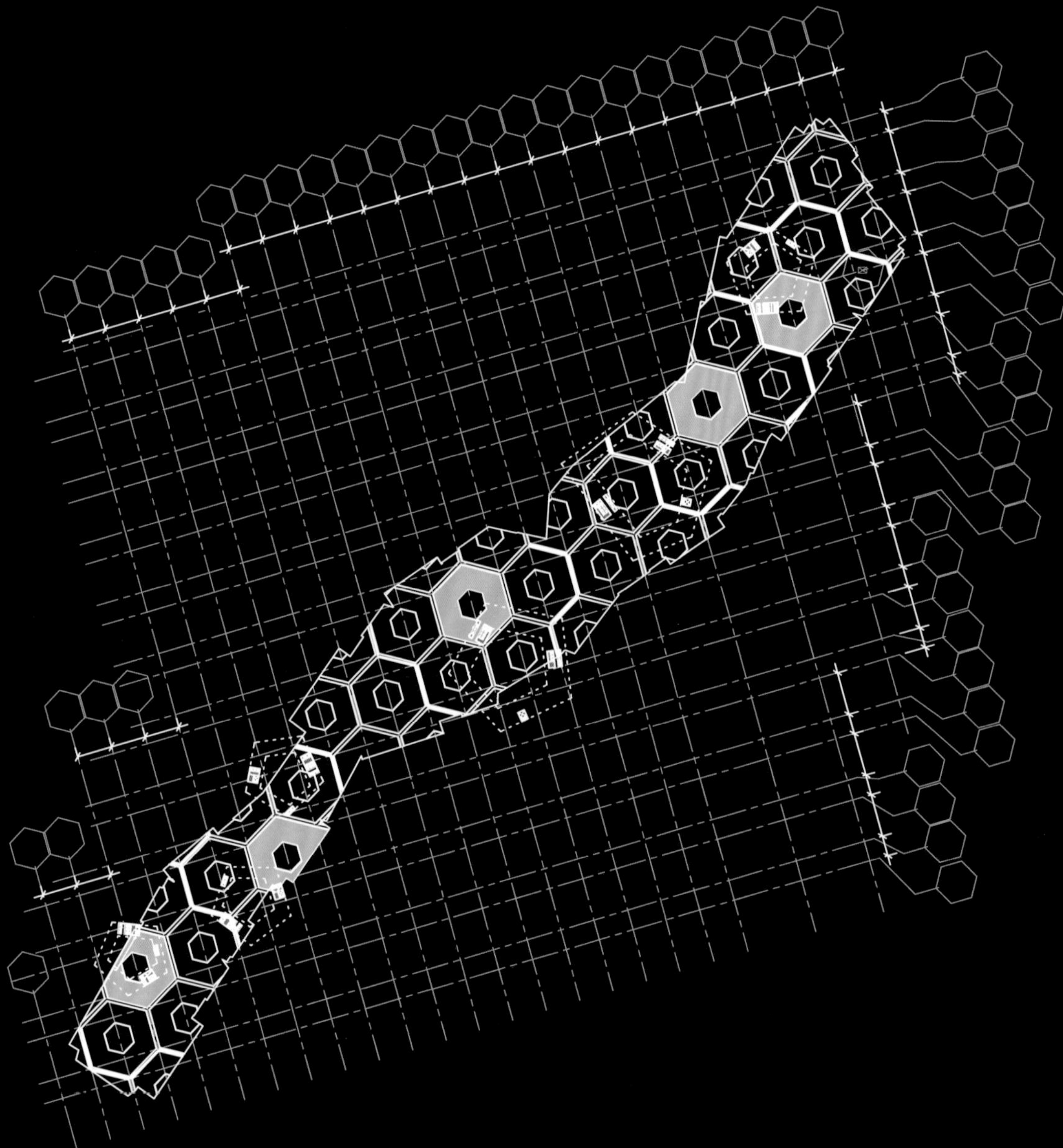

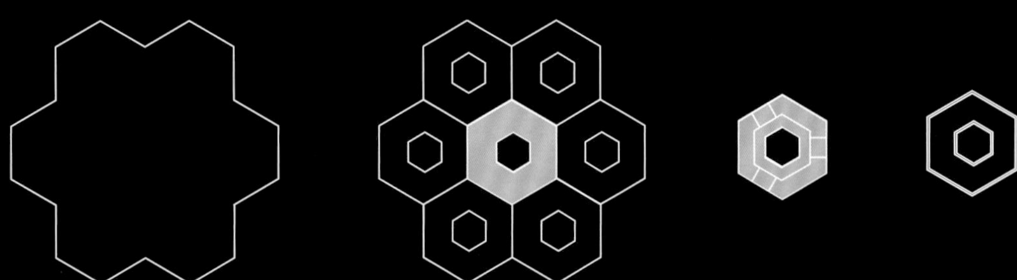

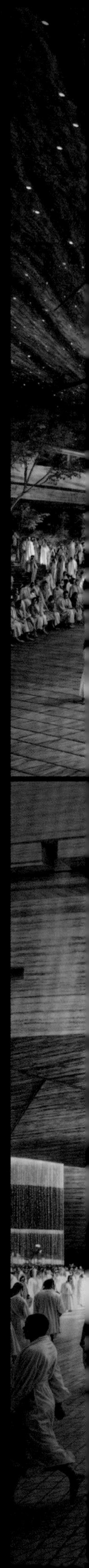

A MODERN, SACRED SITE: The Al Rabita project is comprised of three connected districts that honor the sacredness, history, and natural landscape of Mina, Saudi Arabia. The buildings' hexagonal geometric base forms are directly inspired by the tectonics of the surrounding Hijaz Mountain Range. A destination for people making religious pilgrimage in harsh desert conditions, the project includes protected and shaded ground level gathering areas.

RETHINKING WHAT'S POSSIBLE

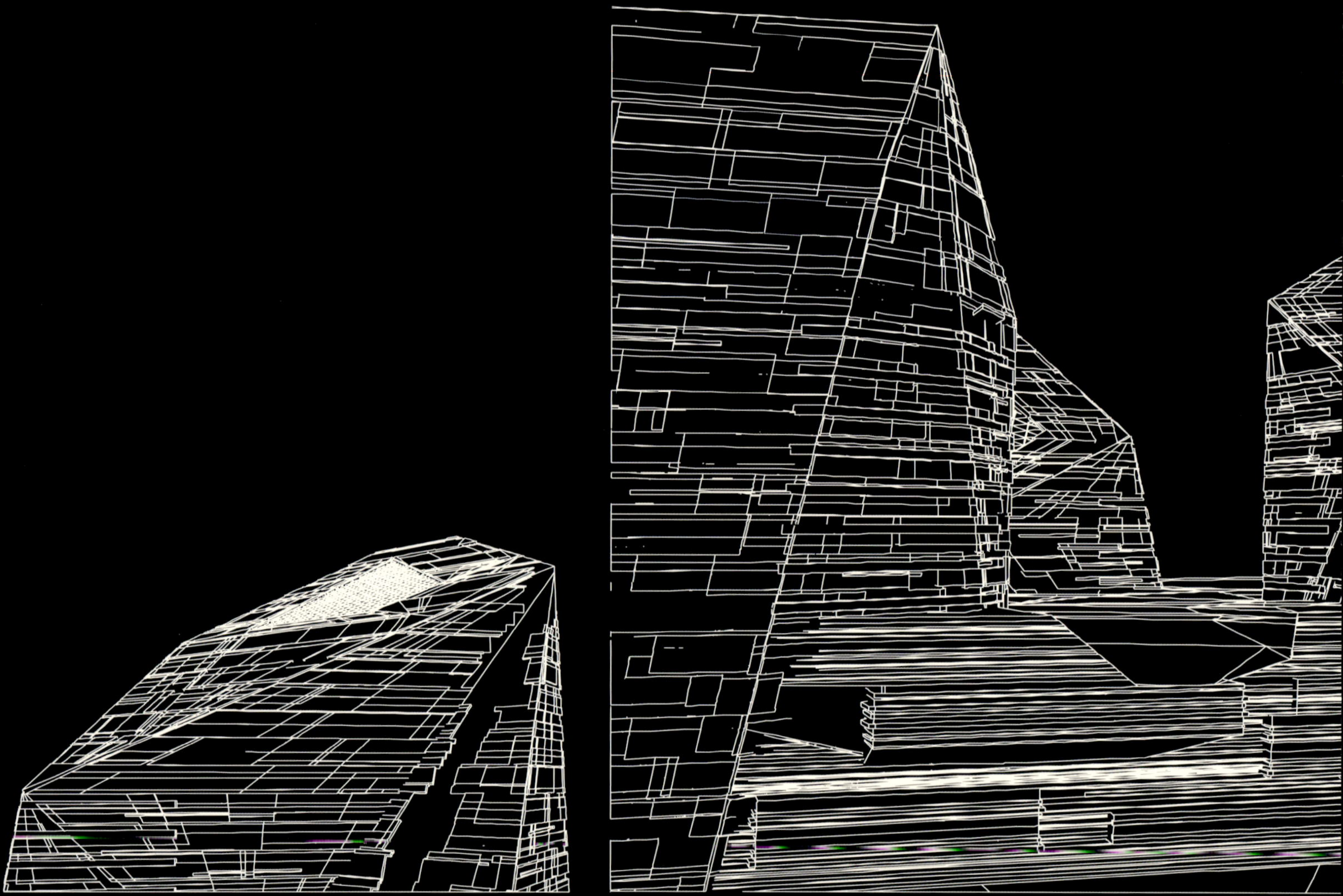

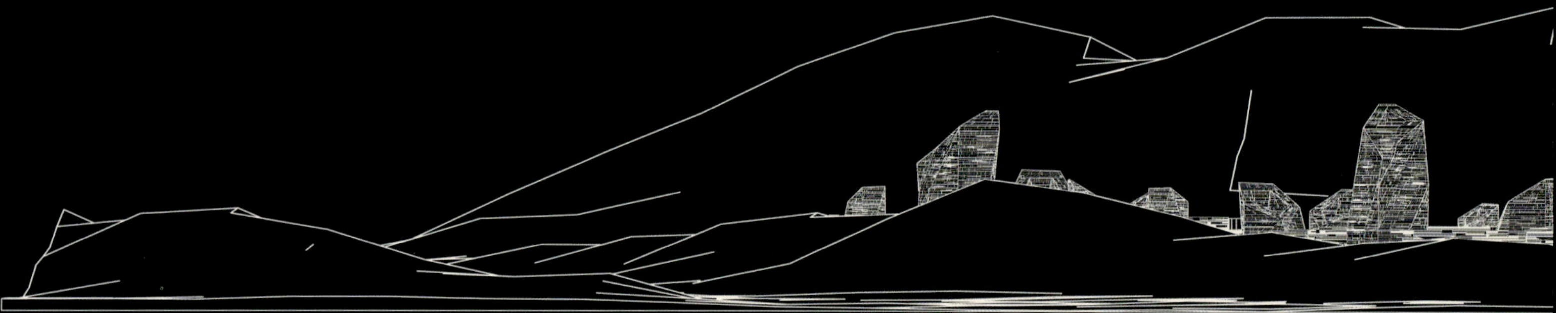

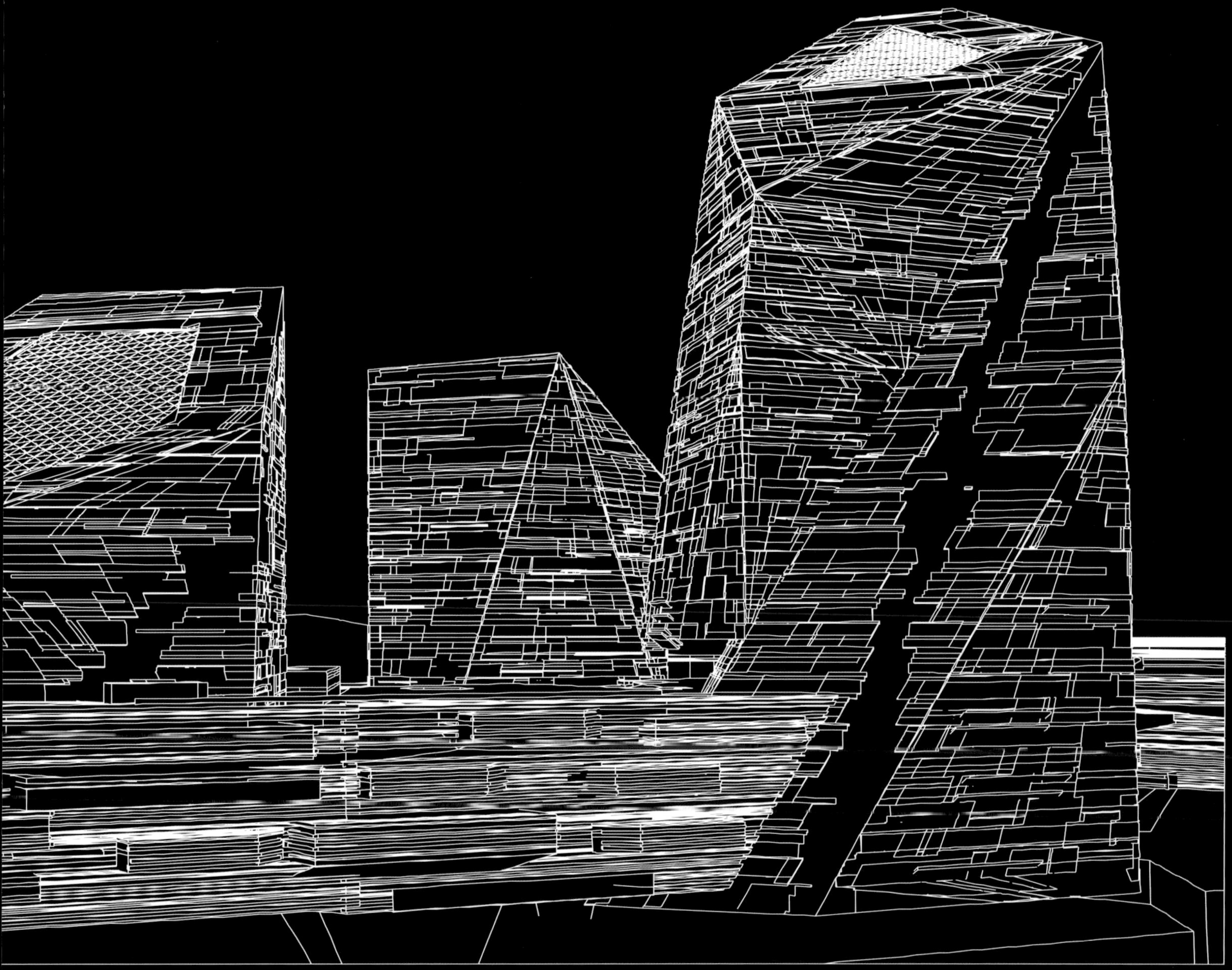

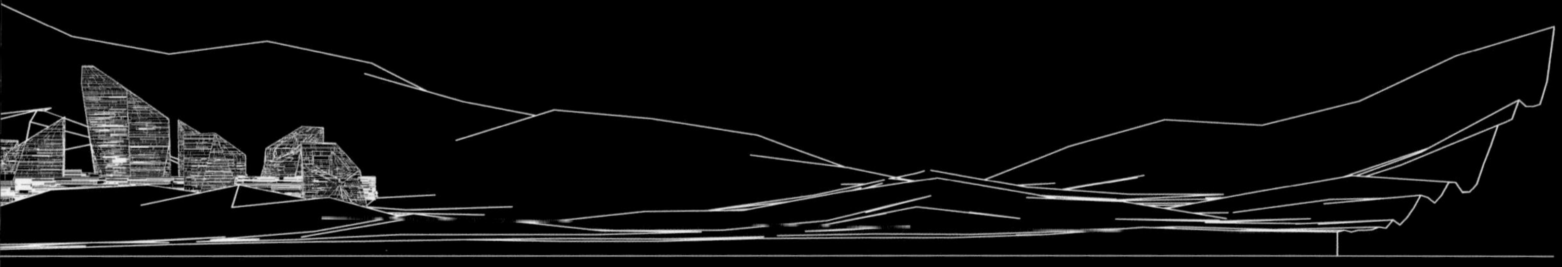

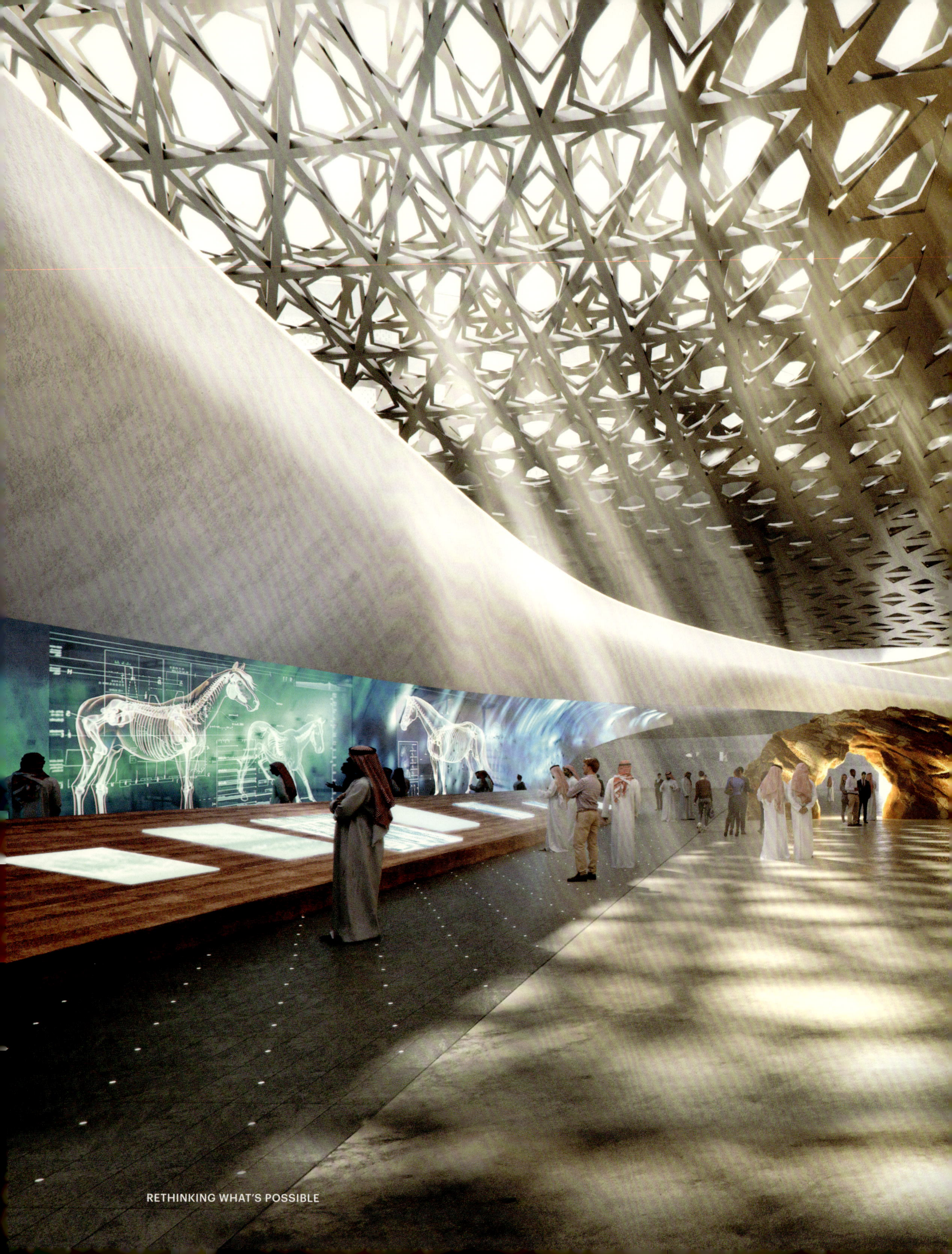

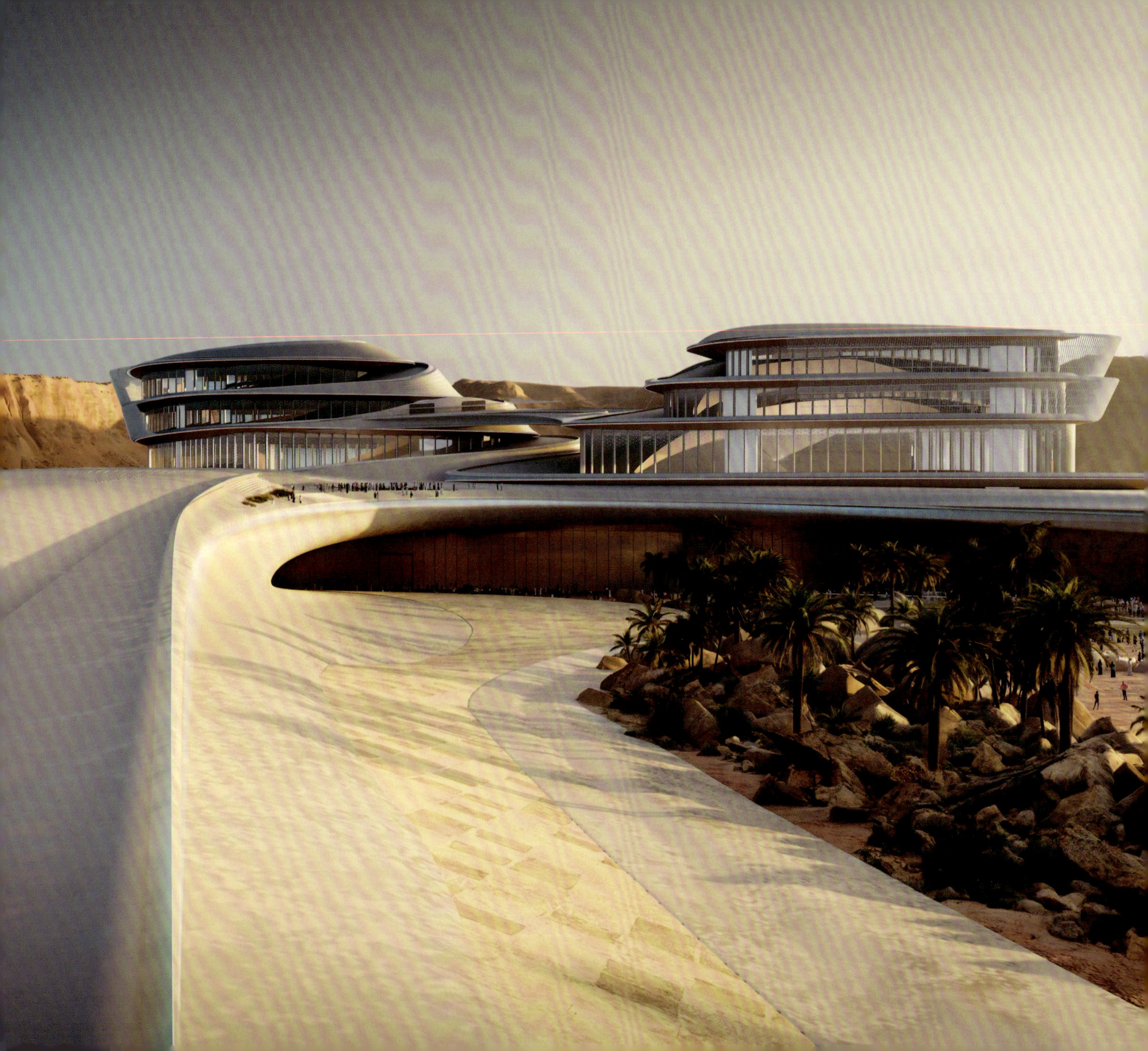

INNOVATING THE GRANDSTAND: In a design competition driven by rethinking what a horseracing grandstand can be, HKS used artificial intelligence tools to generate inspirational imagery using terms related to horses, shapes, and natural elements. Designers used the images as a jumping off point to develop their design solutions for a grandstand of the future.

TEXAS A&M UNIVERSITY
SCHOOL OF LAW

RETHINKING WHAT'S POSSIBLE

SUSTAINABLE DEVELOPMENT: In an effort to reimagine surface parking lots and empty areas on the outskirts of downtown Fort Worth, academia, local government, developers and designers partnered up. The AGRI-LIFE master plan links the Texas A&M campus to downtown with sustainable design and public amenities.

DOSWELL
BUILDING

RETHINKING WHAT'S POSSIBLE

RECOVERING IN PEACE: The Nexus Recovery Center Doswell Building provides a safe haven for women recovering from substance abuse in Dallas. The building features a concrete tilt-wall structural system with custom fluting pattern. The façade will transform over time, as program graduates add stainless steel tokens that symbolize courage, resilience, and hope.

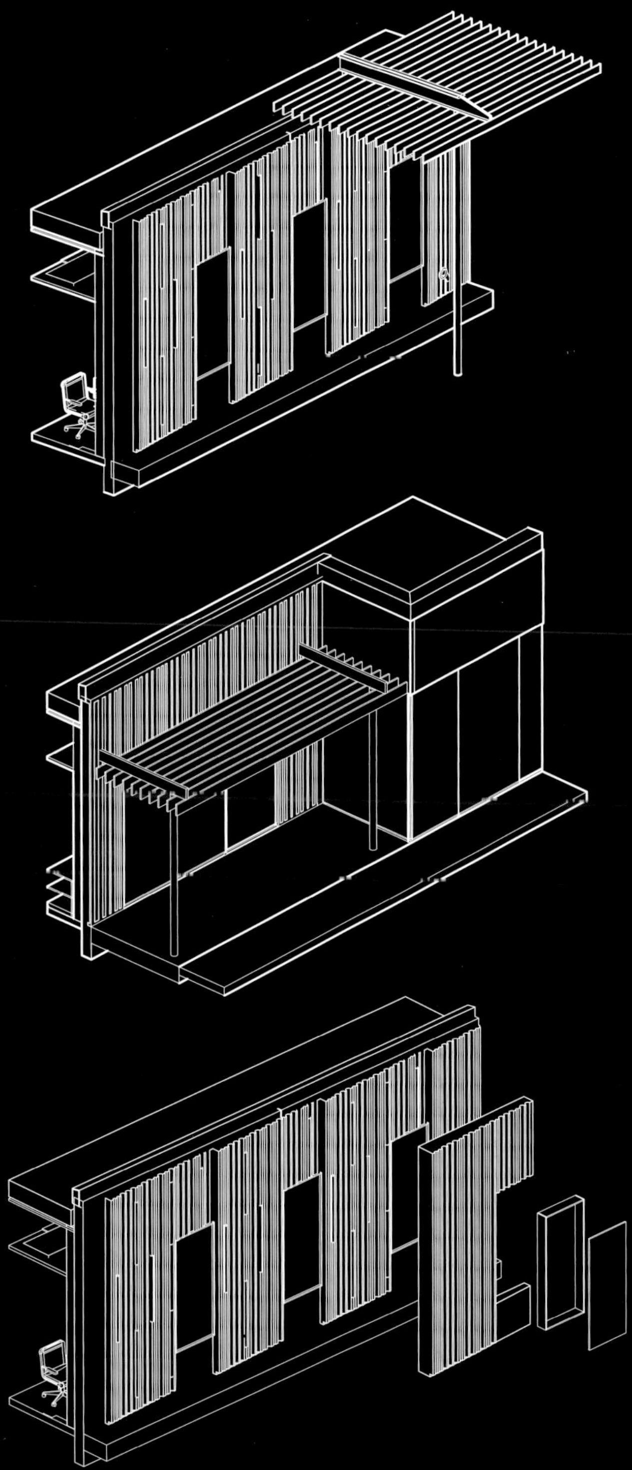

Reception

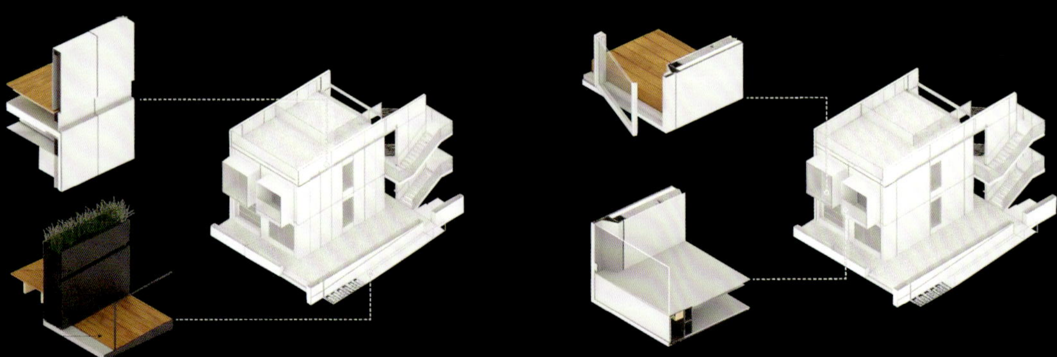

MODULAR FUTURES: HKS partnered with Kasita to design a revolutionary approach to urban living. The stackable, prefabricated microhomes are adaptable and residents can personalize their homes with attachable components such a s stairs, balconies, and solar panels. Delivered by truck and installed by crane, the units can be arranged in various configurations and are intended to address housing shortages and urban density challenges.

PARKING
AREA

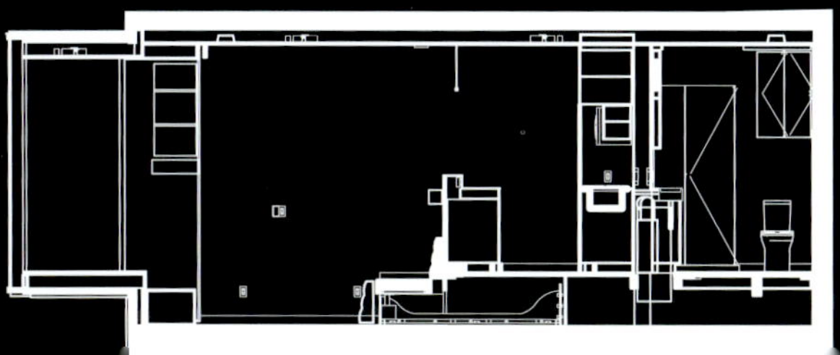

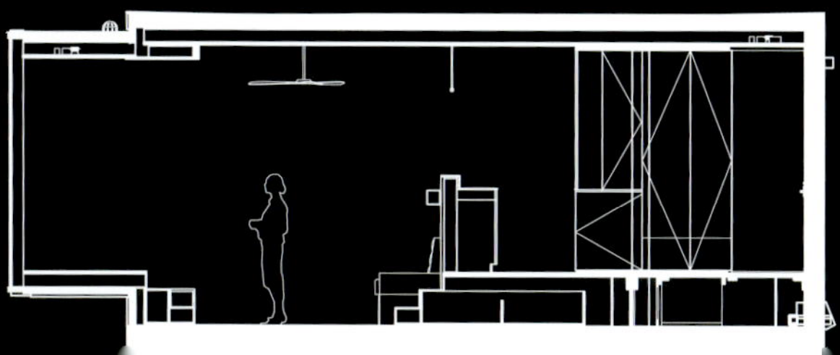

NAVWAR

INTEGRITY
HONOR
COURAGE
COMMITMENT

RETHINKING WHAT'S POSSIBLE

VA EL PASO HEALTH CARE CENTER

RETHINKING WHAT'S POSSIBLE

DO NOT ENTER

PATIENT CARE
Empathy
COMFORT
COMPASSION
Esperanza
ENERGY
Safe

HOSPITAL ENTRANCE
AHN WEXFORD

MATERNITY
Midland Metropolitan University Hospital

3
5
Welcome Centre, Main Reception 5
& Access to all areas
Car Park and Way Out
4

DESIGNED FOR FLEXIBILITY: Midland Metropolitan University Hospital in Birmingham, UK, designed by HKS, Cagni Williams and Sonneman Toon, is the largest acute health care facility within the Sandwell and West Birmingham NHS Trust. Based on a single structural grid, the design accommodates a wide range of clinical and functional spaces that can be easily adapted for future expansion and supports the delivery of new service models and working practices as medical technology and acute healthcare needs evolve.

B
B

Piedmont
Collier

RETHINKING WHAT'S POSSIBLE

RETHINKING WHAT'S POSSIBLE

Image Credits

Pacific Plaza Pavilion
Photography: © Parrach LLC, Parrish Ruiz de Velasco (236–237, 240–241); © HKS Inc, Daryl Shields (238); © SWA, William Tatham (242–243)

StationSoccer
Rendering: © HKS, Inc. (244–245)
Satellite images: Google Earth (245)

COVE™ by DIRTT Treatment Area
Photography: © DIRTT Environmental Solutions Ltd. (246)
Renderings: HKS, Inc. and DIRTT (247)

Sensory Well-being Hub
Photography: © Tom Harris (248 bottom, 250–251); © HKS, Inc. (248 top)

Cosm
Photography: © HKS Inc., Daryl Shields (252–253)
Renderings: © HKS Inc. (255)

HKS Atlanta
Photography: © Garrett Rowland Photography (256, 258–259, 261)

AutoCamp Joshua Tree
Photography: © Matt Kisiday (262–263)

AMAALA Triple Bay Marina Yacht Club
Renderings: © HKS, Inc. (264–269)

Auckland Stadium
Renderings: © HKS, Inc. (270–273)

The Arena in Diriyah
Renderings: © HKS, Inc. (274–279)

Al Rabita
Renderings: © HKS, Inc. (280–287)

Qiddiya Grandstand
Renderings: © HKS, Inc. (288–291)

Texas A&M University AGRI-LIFE
Renderings: © HKS, Inc. (292–297)

Nexus Recovery Center Doswell Building
Renderings: © HKS, Inc. (298–301)

Zev Yaroslavsky Family Support Center
Photography: © HKS, Inc., Blake Marvin (302–305)

Kasita
Renderings: © HKS, Inc. (306–307)

NAVWAR
Renderings: © HKS, Inc. (308–311)

VA El Paso Health Care Center
Rendering: © HKS, Inc. (312–313)

330 N. Clark
Renderings: © HKS, Inc. (314–315)

Allegheny Health Network Wexford Hospital
Photography: © Ed Massery (316–317)

Southern Gateway Park
Renderings: © HKS, Inc. (318–321)

Midland Metropolitan University Hospital
Design: HKS, Inc., Cagni Williams, Sonneman Toon
Photography: © Jack Hobhouse (322–327)

Piedmont Atlanta Hospital Marcus Tower
Photography: © Tom Harris (328–329, 332); © Katie Bricker Photography (330–331)

REFLECTIONS AND ASPIRATIONS

Postscript by Heath May, Forthcoming CEO and Chairman of HKS

In this moment, I reflect on the challenges we have faced and the work we have done, and I am excited for what lies ahead. At HKS, we are poised to step confidently into a future that holds immeasurable opportunity. As we look forward, one thing that is clear: to achieve our ambition, we must all agree that "good enough" is never enough.

The progress we have made in recent decades, the progress demonstrated by the projects and innovations in this book, is palpable. It is a testament to the talent and dedication of everyone at HKS that draws on a legacy of transformation spanning more than eighty-five years. Looking to the decades ahead, I am confident our teams will keep pushing boundaries, driven by the understanding that true innovation often lies beyond our comfort zone.

Our future includes the possibility of industry disruption through technology, a reality we must embrace rather than fear. We have the power to shape what lies ahead and expand our definition of design to elevate our work and its impact on the world.

We are one team at HKS, a team comprised of myriad skillsets and incredible depth. This ethos is embedded in our design process, and it will carry us forward. By fostering a culture of collective curiosity and continuous learning, we position ourselves to thrive. We will leverage technology in a way that aligns with our values. We will anticipate trends and navigate disruption with agility. As we stand on the precipice of holistic digital transformation, HKS has the talent, vision, and drive to lead the industry. I see the challenges we will face as opportunities to redefine what is possible. With this mindset, we envision a future guided by HKS' core values of relationships, character, and purpose.

Looking back is not about nostalgia; it is about understanding. It is about seeing the threads that connect our values to our actions. When I survey our history, I see resilience, adaptability, and innovation. From our earliest work to the projects on the boards today, each and every step has yielded growth. The lessons learned from our past—successes and failures—serve as a reminder that little is achieved without calculated risk.

Looking forward, I am filled with optimism. The opportunities before us are immense. This moment calls for clarity of purpose and unity of action. We will not sit back and observe as the world and our industry transform around us. We will face the change with curiosity and determination. Together, we will shape a future that reflects the best of who we are and who we aspire to be.

To look back is to learn, and to look forward is to lead. I am excited about what we will imagine and accomplish together.

Project Index

ORO EDITIONS
PUBLISHERS OF ARCHITECTURE, ART, AND DESIGN
GORDON GOFF: PUBLISHER

WWW.OROEDITIONS.COM
INFO@OROEDITIONS.COM

PUBLISHED BY ORO EDITIONS

Directors: Dan Noble, FAIA, FACHA; Heath May, FAIA
Preface: James P. Cramer, Hon. AIA, Hon. IIDA
Editors: William Richards; Kathleen M. O'Donnell
Editorial Direction: Anthony Montalto, AIA; Upali Nanda, PhD, Assoc AIA, EDAC, ACHE; Ann Kifer; Shalmir Johnston; Julie Obiala
Creative Director: James Frisbie
Graphic Designers/Illustrators: Estefania Larragoity; Jaya Tolefree

10 9 8 7 6 5 4 3 2 1
FIRST EDITION

ISBN: 978-1-961856-65-3

PREPRESS AND PRINT WORK BY ORO EDITIONS INC.
PRINTED IN CHINA

ORO Editions makes a continuous effort to minimize the overall carbon footprint of its publications. As part of this goal, ORO, in association with Global ReLeaf, arranges to plant trees to replace those used in the manufacturing of the paper produced for its books. Global ReLeaf is an international campaign run by American Forests, one of the world's oldest nonprofit conservation organizations. Global ReLeaf is American Forests' education and action program that helps individuals, organizations, agencies, and corporations improve the local and global environment by planting and caring for trees.

Ross and JW Marriott Dallas Arts District; © HKS,